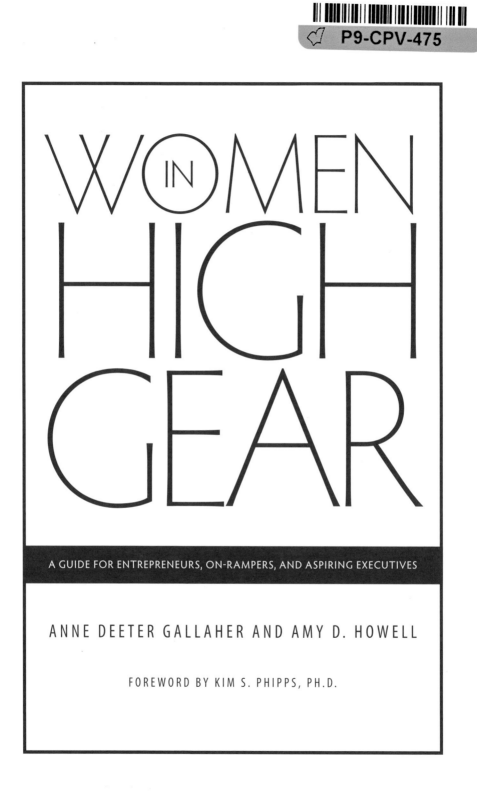

W(IN)OMEN HIGH GEAR

A GUIDE FOR ENTREPRENEURS, ON-RAMPERS, AND ASPIRING EXECUTIVES

ANNE DEETER GALLAHER AND AMY D. HOWELL

FOREWORD BY KIM S. PHIPPS, PH.D.

Printed in the United States of America
First Printing, 2013
ISBN 978-0615781259
www.WomenInHighGear.com
@WomenInHighGear

To women everywhere who have big ideas and a "healthy disregard for the impossible." High gear awaits!

Acclaim

FOR *WOMEN IN HIGH GEAR*

*"This book is for anyone wanting to soar to higher goals
in business. It is a refreshing departure from other how-to books
and full of good stories to get you there."*

PHILIP H. TRENARY

CEO, Phil Trenary Associates; Former CEO, Pinnacle Airlines Corporation

*"*Women in High Gear *speaks to the 20-something personally and
professionally without the undertones of a lecturing parent or mentor.
Exploring the C-suite opportunities for females, Anne and Amy prove
that nothing is unattainable for the focus-driven woman with hard work,
practice development, and a little elbow grease.* Women in High Gear
*is the modern guide to overcoming obstacles and achieving success
without breaking a sweat—and doing it all in 4-inch heels.
Anne and Amy have hit a homerun!"*

KAITLIN SAWYER

Public Relations/Marketing Professional, Hawaii

*"In a business world steeped in too much self-help blather,
Amy and Anne stand up for accountability, distinctiveness, mental
toughness, responsibility, hard work, compassion, and appropriate
compromise—the values that forge great leaders. This book is
inspiring, true, and even better—entertaining!"*

MARK W. SCHAEFER

College Educator, Entrepreneur, International Speaker, and
Author of *Return on Influence* and *The Tao of Twitter*

"Women in High Gear is proof of the power of storytelling—at which Anne Deeter Gallaher and Amy D. Howell excel. They turn their hard-won personal and professional experiences into illuminating and engaging examples for others to follow. Early and mid-career professionals will find High Gear immediately useful, but even seasoned executives (like me) will see in Amy and Anne's experiences new approaches to today's challenges."

KATHLEEN A. PAVELKO
President/CEO, WITF, Harrisburg, PA

"The collective 40-plus years of High Gear expertise that wonder duo of Anne and Amy pack into this book is unmatched. Inspiring and educational, this book is brimming with proof of how modern-day women can navigate their way to the C-suite and become admired business leaders. Integrating the fresh world of social media into their marketing mix has allowed these two treasures to become worldwide marketing resources and has given them the attention they so rightly deserve. Reading about how these ladies have overcome the hurdles of owning their own companies, parenthood, and glass ceilings provides valuable insight into how independent, driven women can dominate the professional business landscape."

SUSAN R. EWING
Director of Social & Digital Media, Hershey Harrisburg Regional Visitors Bureau

"In Women in High Gear, Anne and Amy come together to weave in intricate detail a complete and realistic picture of the successful business woman. Through a powerful mix of humor, professionalism, and valuable lessons learned firsthand, the two have created an invaluable handbook for women in any stage of their career. The book discusses the tools essential to building a successful career, from learning to accept a compliment and building emotional resilience to networking for business and developing a brand. Anne and Amy candidly share their stories of balancing a career and a family, overcoming roadblocks, and defining their own high gear. After reading, I immediately wrote out my high gear goals for the next five years. This book is for any woman with a big dream for her life!"

RACHAEL DYMSKI
Author

Table of Contents

Foreword

BY KIM S. PHIPPS, PH.D.
PRESIDENT, MESSIAH COLLEGE

When I consider women who have achieved the seemingly impossible, I think of my maternal grandmother, Sophie. Her example as a woman of boldness and strength continues to inspire me. At the age of 21, my grandmother bravely set sail from Germany destined for New York City and for what she hoped would be a fresh start and a new adventure. Unable to speak English, she traveled alone with a handwritten note and the address of a German family for whom she would serve as maid and cook. To learn the language of her newly adopted country, she went to the movies every weekend. I cannot imagine the courage it took for her to leave everything that was familiar and travel to the unfamiliar.

Stories of daring women like my grandmother encourage and challenge me as I serve as president of Messiah College. In my experience, operating in high gear means wholeheartedly following my passions for faith, people, and learning. I pursue these passions by devoting myself to spending time with my family, serving the broader community, and leading and advancing the mission of an institution to which I'm deeply committed. As a college administrator, I have the privilege of interacting with students and helping to prepare them for lives of leadership, service, and reconciliation in the 21st century.

Anne Deeter Gallaher and Amy D. Howell are also keenly attuned to the need for mentoring, guidance, and inspiration to help prepare current and future generations of women for leadership in business and society. In *Women in High Gear*, Anne and Amy have artfully woven their own high gear journeys to both mark a path for growth and to steer readers clear of roadblocks. They blend advice, personal experience, insight, and accountability in hopes of shortening the learning curves of other women.

I was honored to be part of the "Women in High Gear" panel that helped launch this book project. Not only did I enjoy interacting with the distinguished group of executives Anne assembled, but I also was impressed with her passion and drive to help other women to network and pursue their most ambitious goals while also balancing commitments to family and community.

I believe in the transformative power of women sharing their life stories and experiences of leadership. As women, we live in a season of opportunity and expectation. My grandmother would be amazed at where our passions can lead us. These are exhilarating times to be in business, begin a career, or relaunch ourselves after a sabbatical. *Women in High Gear* will challenge, inspire, and guide women at all stages of career development to set priorities, overcome obstacles, and achieve their boldest goals and callings.

Preface

In a 2012 McKinsey study for *The Wall Street Journal*, *Unlocking the Full Potential of Women at Work*, 41% of successful women polled aspired to the C-suite, a chief executive position. "I enjoy creating a workplace—making the decisions that affect people's lives for the better." "I want a seat at the table."

The talent, robust work ethic, negotiating skills, and financial acumen to lead a business and to lead people is acquired from many experiences—not all of these are learned in college. In fact, neither of us have degrees in business; we are professional communicators.

Whether you work for a Fortune 500 company or for a small business, your high gear is within reach. As we serve on boards of directors, lead community initiatives, and raise children, we hope our work-life experiences and career trajectories provide an incentive for you to set your goals for success and shift into high gear.

Introduction

Recessions and depressions, slowdowns and rallies are part of American business life. Each downturn and recovery gives us an opportunity to study the DNA in companies that have thrived, and to gain insight from them.

What types of leaders and business owners survived? What types of companies adapted and remained profitable? How did small business respond to regulation, policy, and the new normal? Who shifted into high gear?

As owners of marketing and public relations firms, the two of us work in an industry particularly hard hit during recessions. Budgets were slashed, marketing investments stalled, and social media took the world by storm and surprise. We both realized, however, that now was an opportunity to be an outlier. For us, it was a season to understand and harness the power of digital and social media. We persuaded our clients to invest more resources into marketing and public relations and not to simply treat these as line items on the company budget.

In separate states with separate business models, we joined Twitter in 2009 and our companies have been transformed. We had high gear goals for our businesses before, but social media afforded us a new tool in our Influencer kit. We immediately realized its potential to be a game changer for our clients and for our own businesses.

Although we are similar in services offered and core values, we are personally dissimilar in how we came to entrepreneurship, and how we each have shifted into high gear. The good news is that there is no better time for women to succeed in business; there's no better time for entrepreneurs as well.

Whatever your measure of success—profitability, financial independence, economic growth, competitiveness, influence, affluence—it's time to shift into high gear. One of our favorite quotes is from Jonathan Winters, "If your ship doesn't come in, swim to it!" We invite you to join us—the water's fine!

We are writing from a female lens—as businesswomen, wives, and mothers—but we also share a commitment with most of our male business counterparts in our zeal to do better business and to make a difference every day.

We really believe men, women, students, retirees, Millennials, Boomers, and on-rampers will gain something from our experiences. **It's our desire that our stories and the paths to our business success will shorten your own learning curves.**

How far you rise in leadership and influence, and how successful you are depends first on you. We believe strongly in a No Whining zone. If you find yourself falling back on these thought patterns or blaming others for your career stalls, this book will help you get past those barriers. We don't accept the blame game. Rather, we champion relentless hard work, strategic goal setting, genuine relationship building, and an iron-clad belief in yourself.

We are not saying there aren't people who will try to thwart your success or pass you over for a promotion (it has happened to us); people who will gossip and devalue your services; women who will resent your climb—these are business realities. You will learn to overcome them. If you hit a ceiling—glass, steel, self-imposed—don't let it hold you back. Reroute. If you don't like the ground rules in the company you work for, channel your energy into positive change. It may be time to build your own sandbox.

One of our foundations for success is to love what you do. Thomas Edison said, "I never did a day's work in my life! It was all fun!" We agree.

CHAPTER 1
Defining High Gear

"The essence of America—that which really unites us—is not ethnicity, or nationality, or religion—it is an idea—and what an idea it is: That you can come from humble circumstances and do great things."

CONDOLEEZZA RICE

Successful leaders are inherent strategists. They think big. They have ideas. They know where the goal line is. You can't chart a course to nowhere and expect to arrive at an amazing destination. What exactly is high gear? Our high gear may be different than yours, to be sure. We don't all aspire to be Marissa Mayer, CEO of Yahoo!, or Sheryl Sandberg, COO of Facebook, or Condoleezza Rice, former United States Secretary of State.

But if you're reading this book, you probably do aspire to make a difference in the world, reach financial independence, or attain a leadership position in your organization. Your high gear might be a six-figure income, or a C-suite position. If you're working for someone else, high gear might be the opportunity to start your own business, buy out your competitor, or achieve your impossible.

This book is meant to be a help to women everywhere who desire better for themselves and their families. It will help you think in high gear and gain insight into how two women are achieving high gear in business and life. We believe strongly in helping others advance, both women and men. Whether you're using your strengths as a teacher, an entrepreneur, or an executive, the world needs the benefits of your high gear.

ANNE

Let's begin by defining what high gear is for you. When I was working for a publishing company, my high gear was a management position in a company that was nearly 100 years old and had never had a female manager. Once I achieved that, my new high gear was to create a work-from-home position when I took maternity leave. The company had never provided that for any employee, but I don't believe anyone ever asked either. After 15 years of working from home, my next high gear was my longest shot yet—to start my own company. Your high gear will be a metamorphosis, too, and it may shift and change with the seasons of your life.

As an entrepreneur, I set my sights on building a highly valued service business with successful clients. I also set an income goal. In my world it was big, and my accountant would remind me that big numbers are good until you have to pay big taxes on your success. In 2000, my high gear income goal seemed like a crazy high number. But the harder I worked and the more I networked, the less out-of-reach the goal became. Once I reached that goal, I set a new one and added a revenue goal.

Now I've added achievements to my high gear goals—to have myself and my clients published in the national media, to be a leader in social media communications, and to write a book. I'll never forget the conversation I had with Ford CEO Alan Mulally that defined a major triumph in my quest for high gear. He was deep into a storyline when he stopped and turned to me with a smile and said, "Don't tweet that, Anne." I suddenly realized I had reached one of my high gear goals and a new level of social media influence.

Whatever your high gear, it begins in your own mind. Set a stretch goal—to develop a product, to earn a quarter of a million dollars in one year, or to disrupt an entire industry—and then create a strategy to accomplish it. High gear women are confident, resilient, and bold. We have a positive inner voice, strong interpersonal skills, and choose our company wisely.

AMY

High gear for me is the point when you attain confidence that comes from staying power in the business world. It's that voice deep down that calls you to action and keeps you focused on your goals. Some people have tried to define me, but I refuse to allow others to define my journey. I have had my share of challenges and with each obstacle you must keep your focus, integrity, and will to stay in high gear. You will need an iron-clad belief in your abilities and your intuition. The two together are a mighty force for high gear.

I have a saying in my firm: "Tell your own story or someone else will." This refers to public relations, but it's true in how we view ourselves, and it sets the stage for how we handle ourselves in boardrooms, executive suites, or carpool lines. Women in high gear have a clear vision of what their story is and a voice strong enough to tell it.

CHAPTER 2
The Journey Depends on You: Our Backstories

"It's part of my personality, probably, that I never give up. I tend to be stubborn. When I make up my mind, I go to the end. It didn't even come to my mind that I would stop."

ROMI HAAN, FOUNDER AND CEO, HAAN CORPORATION

ANNE

I grew up in a family of entrepreneurs. My career began in 1981 as an editorial assistant in a Christian publishing house. I started work on the Monday after my Saturday college graduation. This was my first job interview, and I was offered the position. I was getting married in a month so my goal was to get a job. If it was in my major, that was all the better.

My salary was $10,500 a year, and I was feeling very accomplished and important. I was also totally unprepared for office politics and management hierarchy. On my first day, my boss asked me to make the coffee shortly after I arrived in the office. *Are you kidding me?* I thought. I had just graduated from college with a Bachelor's in English and a Bachelor's in Communications/Journalism—with honors. Surely I knew everything. This was not in my job description. Lucky for me, I kept my mouth shut, and I made the coffee. It was a valuable work lesson to start my career with and demonstrated to my boss that I could be a team player.

No one is beneath making the coffee in an office. I looked at my paycheck and took special notice of who signed it. Whatever he asked me to do (barring any immoral or unethical request), I would do it and be grateful for the job. It was that simple. I was in their sandbox, and I had a lot to learn. At the age of 21, I did not have a clear high gear goal, nor had I given my career path much strategic thought. But that didn't preclude me from reaching several high gears later after a career off-ramp and on-ramp.

Was the job perfect? No, but I had a wonderful 60-year-old mentor who was the editor's secretary. And the editor in chief was a kind, smart man whom I respected. I remember handing him some copy I had written. He read it and handed it back to me. "You can do better," he said.

My feelings were hurt (I would later learn that there's no place for that if you're considering high gear!), and I felt stupid. But it was the best thing he could have done. He pushed me to fine tune my work until it was work I could be very proud of. Even now, every time I write copy for a client, I ask myself, "Is this my best work?" And I also press my employees to rewrite and rework until their efforts are the best efforts.

Crammed into the editorial offices in an old city building, I started to forge my path as a young and very inexperienced businesswoman. Was there a glass ceiling? Yes. Was it impenetrable? No. Were there inequities in the workplace? Absolutely.

Soon after I began, I encountered my first inequity, and it was with my benefits package. My husband was finishing his senior year in college, and I was the only wage earner. I realized that he wasn't covered on my health insurance, but the wives and families of the male employees were all covered with health insurance. *That's not fair*, I thought.

I scheduled a meeting with my boss to share my concern and to ask for a fair resolution. I was careful not to be aggressive. I gathered my facts and asked for an audience. That's when I learned that my predecessor had left the position for that same reason. Her husband was self-employed, and the company had not included him on her benefits package either. I spoke with clarity and honesty, and they changed the policy.

Although I was an entry-level worker in the office, I wanted to add value and bring new ideas. Early on, I asked to go to editorial conferences so I could learn new skills and make our editorial department sharper. I entered our publications in national contests where the editorial team was recognized for communication skills.

My first recollection of striving for high gear was on a cookbook project in 1985. *Foreign Flavors* was a cookbook compiled from missionaries around the world. Our staff collected (through the mail!), organized, indexed, edited, proofed, typeset, and printed the cookbook in house. As Director of Editorial Services, I really wanted to include a compelling Foreword. I wanted someone of acclaim who could authenticate the recipes and add some culinary stardom.

I had had several dinners at The Hotel Hershey and had been introduced to the Executive Chef, Heinz Hautle. He had a warm, charming personality and would stop at our table to say hello on occasion. His sincerity was impressive. Routinely, he would ask about our service and the quality of the meal because he cared— I was no one of importance.

I was excited to tell Betty, the secretary: "I have just the person! We'll ask Heinz Hautle at The Hotel Hershey. The entire world has heard of Hershey's Chocolate. Imagine what that will do for the cookbook and for PR!"

Betty gave me an immediate disapproving look. "He'll never do it," she said shaking her head. I was surprised at how quickly she cut me off. I couldn't figure out if she truly didn't think the idea was worthwhile, or if she doubted I could persuade a world-renowned chef to add his expertise to our missionary cookbook. I was only 25 and had lots of big ideas. Betty was 60, a wonderful lady, but she had no big ideas. Nor was she a supporter of big ideas. If I was going to try this it would be on my own and without her support.

A few weeks later, armed with a healthy dose of self-talk and confidence, I scheduled a meeting with The Hotel Hershey's Executive Chef and left a page-proof copy of the 239-page cookbook in the hotel's kitchen. Not only did *Foreign Flavors* go to press with a glowing Foreword, but it carried the signatures of the Executive Chef, two Chefs de Cuisine, and the Chef Pâtissier. I didn't realize it then, but this was a shift into high gear.

The first step on the road to high gear is to believe in yourself. If you don't believe you have a worthwhile idea or the ability to make it happen, don't expect anyone else to go to war with you. My father's lifetime principle was "Nothing ventured, nothing gained!" I put that adage into action in 2000 when I started my own business. That was a milestone in my high gear journey.

While working part-time from home and raising our three sons, I realized that the business world would pay well for good writing and good marketing materials. I also decided that if I was going to be away from my family, it would have to be for the highest amount of money that the market would bear. And that meant I would need to work for myself. The caveats were that I had never started a business, I never took any business courses in college, and I was 40 years old. That's not exactly a solid business model to take to the bank. But, I set up shop with a computer in our bedroom, called it my office, on-ramped, and never looked back.

Thirteen years later, my high gear is office space with employees. I was honored as one of Pennsylvania's Best Women in Business; I have been published in *The Wall Street Journal*, am a member of *The Wall Street Journal* Women in the Economy Task Force, have learned from and visited with Ford CEO Alan Mulally in Dearborn, and am collaborating with *New York Times* #1 Best-Selling author Keith Ferrazzi on a podcast.

In 2013, I expanded our services into Nashville, Tennessee, and am pursuing more clients in the music entertainment industry. And now I'm crossing book author off my bucket list.

In *Who's Got Your Back*, Keith Ferrazzi recounts a story where one of his personal advisors is challenging him to channel his motivation better: "Define your greatness. And as soon as you do, be convinced of it and start acting like it. Like, really acting like it. Someone will notice and buy into you and your vision, I promise." Sage advice!

If you're serious about business success, then join us. We will share what tools have worked for us, some ideas on how you can leverage them for your own high gear journey, and introduce you to some special people who have helped us along the way.

AMY

I was the oldest of three girls and my family moved around the South for my father's job. He is a retired Presbyterian preacher (yes, I've endured the preacher's kid jokes all my life). In 1974, when I was 10, we moved from Austin in the great state of Texas to Mobile, Alabama. I thought I had moved to a foreign country, and everyone in Mobile made fun of our Texas accents. It wasn't long before my Dad became one of the best-known preachers in the region, and our family was warmly welcomed. You won't find more gracious, southern Christian people than those in Mobile.

My parents quickly made wonderful friends, and soon I was learning to saltwater fish, hunt, and shoot with the best-of-the-best. In 1976, we were in the Gulf of Mexico catching cobia near an oil rig, and our host and beloved hunt master, Dr. William Rowell, still alive at age 92, said to me and my sister, "Ya'll girls aren't afraid to go in a bucket are you? Because ya'll don't have a water pistol, and y'all can't get in the water out here."

Momentarily stunned because I had no brothers and no grown man had ever said anything like that to me, I recovered and said, "No sir, we can go in a bucket; no problem." I will never forget those precious times outdoors with my Dad. Some of our best conversations have been shared over bass fishing in Onion Creek in Texas and saltwater fishing in the Gulf. It was in those moments that I was preparing for high gear.

Being a self-starter is a gift and a blessing, often in disguise. I was always finding ways around barriers. I had a job at 15 and passed a horrid water safety course on the Navy base (they may have well been SEALS) to become a lifeguard in the summers. Only a few teens passed. This was one of my earliest high gear moments and it had a lasting impression.

Even today, thinking about the final test, my heart races a little. My instructor told us to go tread water in the 15-foot deep end, turn around and face the other way, and prepare to be attacked.

To pass the test, we had to tread as long as they wanted us to. In my case, it was at least 30 minutes. At any point, they could come from behind, grab you, and try their best to take you under, and ultimately prove you couldn't win the struggle. But determined and stubborn—or "hell bent" as we like to say in the South—I passed. It never occurred to me that I couldn't or wouldn't pass. Once you have that mindset, you can reach high gear.

I learned the valuable skill of using my long fingernails and pulling hair. I also knew a few well-placed kicks could render a man still enough for me to get him in a cross-carry position in the water— all 250 lbs. and 6 feet of him.

As I was carrying him across the pool, I was still yanking on his chest hair. He said to me: "You pass. Now let go." To which I replied, "Not on your life, and if you roll or try to get away, I promise I'll pull it out." That experience gave me confidence as a young girl in a world dominated by men in almost every field. It also paved the way for me to lifeguard at the area's best pools, teach swimming lessons to over 100 kids, and meet some of the most influential businessmen who would later steer me to Rhodes College.

I sailed through Murphy High School in Mobile, Alabama, making friends and taking my AP classes seriously. I had a great teacher, Ms. Welborn, who ultimately led me to major in English and find a career where I could use my writing and communications skills.

We can never underestimate the value and impact our teachers have on our kids, especially in high school. I became the first female in the history of the high school to be President of the Key Club. I guess I thought I was an overachiever when in reality, I was just understanding that my journey depended on nobody but me. In my senior year, my friends were being tagged as "prettiest" and "most likely to succeed," and I was tagged with the Daughters of American Revolution Good Citizenship award. At the time, I was a bit mystified by this but later appreciated the impact and meaning of that award.

My parents drilled it into me that I could and should do whatever I wanted to do. My Mom told me early on that I needed to find a career where I could call the shots. Lifeguarding was the perfect high school job and my family teased me (still do) about always having the clipboard and whistle in hand. My thoughts then were, "Hey, somebody's got to be in charge and it might as well be me." These early successes in high school and later in college helped me build my confidence and learn that I had to plow ahead and find my way regardless of what others said and did.

I began to realize this early in my career. As the administrative/ marketing assistant to the CEO of a large architectural firm, I was truly lowest on the totem pole—even with a freshly inked BA from Rhodes College. I was basically the chief gopher. I cleaned the kitchen, ordered sandwiches, cleaned up after meetings, organized a move, did inventory, took notes, and typed them on a typewriter.

Often I found myself staying at the office until 8 or 9 p.m. to catch up on the more serious work I wanted to do. I read everything I could find (this was 1986 before the Internet), and I asked to sit in on as many meetings as I could to take notes. Actually, I wanted to know what was going on. I learned that by taking notes (viewed then by men as what we women did), I was in on the strategy sessions. The more I knew, the more I could contribute. It wasn't long before my CEO was asking me to do more complex tasks and involving me in more strategy sessions. I was shifting into a higher gear, and I liked it.

One day, the firm was submitting a proposal to the German government to design health care facilities on military bases. This was in 1988 before we really had modern computers; our work was performed on electronic typewriters mostly. Often my days were spent tediously typing (or re-typing) documents on forms—255s and 254s. We were in a race to the deadline and as people started leaving the office to go home, I was thinking, "How can they just leave when we have to submit this proposal by midnight via FedEx?"

A few people stayed, and I ended up being tapped to hand deliver the stack of freshly bound proposals to FedEx just before midnight at the Memphis International Airport. Also, I knew it was vital that it get there, and I probably didn't trust anybody else to get it there. High gear means stepping up and doing what nobody else wants to or has the will to do. It means having skin in the game— ownership of whatever task is in front of you.

The firm was successful in winning the work and that started years of work in Germany for us. Looking back, the lessons are vast, and I am grateful for every small detail and every bit of that grunt work.

Your journey depends on how you decide to view your work. For me, I knew I had to work harder, be the gopher, and pay my dues. I was investing in myself. When people my age left the office at 5 p.m., I was just getting started. I had decided at age 22 that I was going to have a career—NOT a job. There's a difference.

CHAPTER 3

On-Ramper, Working Mom, or Working Woman

"No one gets to the corner office by sitting on the side, not at the table."

SHERYL SANDBERG, COO, FACEBOOK, TEDWOMEN

ANNE

The *Harvard Business Review* calls me an on-ramper: someone who steps off the career path to raise children or pursue education or research, and then on-ramps. The data on women in the workplace clearly demonstrates our economic power, but it doesn't accurately depict the inner struggles we battle with career decisions—should we stay home, should we try to balance work-home, does balance even exist, what are the health risks of stress, how are schools affected, how are our children affected, how does corporate view this decision, how do other women view this decision?

A Pew Research report from December 2011 illuminated a shift in values. For women ages 18–34, the percentage has climbed for those feeling that a "high paying career is very important" to 66 percent. For men, it's 59 percent. The desire to be a good parent skyrocketed and may indicate a culture change. The era of Supermom is over— 94 percent of women believe that parenthood is "very important," and 91 percent of men say the same.

We're also seeing a shift in the college graduate ratios across gender lines. "For the first time in American history, there are now one million more female college graduates than male. As recently as 2000, it was the opposite…It is pretty clear that in a global, information-based economy where most of the higher paying new jobs will require some degree of higher education, women will have an advantage." ("When It Comes to Education, Men Are Getting Schooled," *AdAge*, February 15, 2011.)

Whatever trends are reported from news desks or at women's and diversity conferences, a decision to return to work or to stay at home after the birth of a child is an intensely personal decision— and on all fronts it has consequences. Every woman must find the best possible option for herself and her family. There is no one-answer-fits-all, and for many women, there is no choice but to return to work full-time. Thankfully, in today's networked business environment, working remotely has become a viable alternative and fits nicely into the parenting season of life. (Not that we ever outgrow that season of life!)

For me, I didn't need convincing. I felt that my 20s and 30s were the season of children. My talents and skills would be unleashed full time at home raising our three sons. In our middle-class neighborhood, where we walked our children to the elementary school, most of the moms were college-educated and stayed home to raise the children. We all helped each other.

Our decision impacted the school musicals, the Scouts, the PTA— we threw ourselves into enriching the school activities and after-school experiences. My lens was never "Should I stay home?," but "How can I stay home? How can we do this on one income?"

It's a big financial decision. In our case, it meant that my husband, who is a high school chemistry teacher, started his own ceramic tile business and worked two jobs. That enabled me to stay at home. Our core belief was that there are no do-overs with our sons. We felt we had the skills to earn more money, but we could never buy time—the ultimate non-renewable resource. The trade-off was foregoing a bigger house, dinners out, newer cars, jewelry, cruises, and extra money in the bank.

After five years at the publishing house and six months pregnant with our first son, Joshua, I proposed a work-at-home option that would allow me to keep my hand in editorial work, come into the office for meetings, and still add to our family's bottom line. It was 1986 and while this type of arrangement wasn't groundbreaking, it was unusual in the non-profit world I worked in.

No one had brokered this type of an arrangement, but that didn't prevent me from framing the opportunity and asking the CEO. Just because the company doesn't have a policy on working remotely or shared work time, doesn't mean you can't research the opportunities and present the case. Thankfully, the company loved the idea, and it was a good off-ramp option for me.

My experiences at home as CEO of the family and church/school volunteer prepared me for the business world in many ways. Have you ever tried to get three, very energetic young boys to bed on time? That demands serious negotiating skills—and a healthy dose of patience and clear communication!

Making sure every child had his permission slips signed, homework done, wrestling headgear in the backpack, and make it to guitar lessons on time required project management skills. My leadership skills were fine-tuned during seven years of Cub Scout Den Mother activities, endless church committees, booster club assignments, and as Director of Vacation Bible schools.

Leading an evening Vacation Bible school program for 120 children every June is a big task. I realized that to run a successful week-long Bible school, I needed a captivating theme, friendly, interactive adults to teach, college students to run the games, and very hip praise and worship leaders. Not to mention a church full of children who would choose to attend when so many other activities were viewed as cooler.

All of these experiences required marketing and organizational skills that are the same across industries. It was an excellent training ground for me, and especially meaningful because I had no budget and was receiving no pay. My marketing skills had to be in high gear.

Many times I have heard women remark that they feel they can't off-ramp, because they will lose marketable skills. I found the opposite to be true. No client ever said, "What have you been doing for the past 15 years, Anne?" In fact, when my choice has come up in business conversations, it was as a point of pride, not embarrassment. An off-ramp certainly doesn't mean you will never reach high gear. I started my business at age 40 with no business background and no guarantees of success. My prerequisites? A desire to make a difference and reach high gear.

Sheryl Sandberg, COO of Facebook, explained in a TEDWomen talk that there were 190 heads of state and nine were women; corporate boards seem to be stalled at 15 to 16 percent female; and even at non-profits, women are a mere 20 percent of board make-up. Making sure women know all their options is the best answer to putting females into positions where they thrive as high performers.

AMY

First of all, nothing can prepare you for having a baby. There is no experience like it and while it may seem like the greatest, most miraculous, joyful of occasions, it is also one of the most difficult things you can ever do—period. Nothing prepares you for the sleep deprivation and total neediness of another human being. I would not trade it for anything, but I tell expectant moms—especially those who have to go back to work—get ready! Get help and sleep while you can, because once you have kids, your schedule and your resources are infinitely taxed.

Unlike Anne, I never stopped working when I had my babies. I really didn't have a choice, so I just plowed on through. But I had great bosses, who later became clients, and an ability to manage my time. When I had my first child, Bryan, now 16, I had just started my firm and was still working for the oldest law firm in Memphis, Waring Cox.

So determined to do it all, I converted a closet in my house to a workstation, installed Internet, and answered every email. This was 1996. Holding my sweet baby boy, I knew deep down that even if I wanted to stay home full-time, I couldn't.

My drive to do more was equal to my drive to be a mom. I used to feel guilty about it, but to all you young women out there: *Don't feel guilty.* You can find that balance—especially now with remote work arrangements and huge advances in technology. I quickly learned my babies were better off in "mother's day out" for a few days a week, a few hours at a time, and I found the best solution every working mom needs: A Ruthie.

Finding the perfect home care is critical, and for my family that meant we needed a Ruthie. Ruthie Scott is probably in her late 60s, but she never tells us her age. Ruthie is a woman of God, a woman of absolutely no vices, and from a lineage of Arkansas sharecroppers. She has limited formal education, but she is the smartest woman I know and the toughest person mentally I have ever met.

Ruthie is one of eight children. Most of her siblings are deceased, but she is still going strong. I found Ruthie through a friend when Bryan was five months old. After trying daycare, I realized I wanted someone to come to my house instead. Ruthie rode the bus, and then I started driving her, which made no sense.

One day I asked her, "Ruthie, have you ever driven a car?" To that she said, "On country roads way back in the day." I said, "If I teach you to drive, get you a car, and a driver's license, will you work for me full-time?" Ruthie eventually learned to drive, and she worked for our family for years while the kids were pre-school ages.

My kids adored her, called her Nanny, and when I had dinner meetings with clients, I knew Ruthie was there to feed them until one parent could get home. I did feel guilty until I realized that my kids were just fine. I balanced a lot and paid close attention to making sure I had enough quality time with my kids.

What I learned? *I was a better parent if I had my work time.* My career and my clients made me a better mom. Not to mention the benefit of having an income stream. Ruthie is why I could have it all—she did our laundry, took exceptional care of my kids, and guarded them as if they were her own. Although she no longer works for us regularly, we see her often and she comes and helps me when I need her. If every executive mom could have a Ruthie, every mom could have a better chance at managing the work-life balance.

Another important aspect of balancing a family and a career is to have a supportive spouse. I don't know how single parents do it, and they have my complete respect. It's important to have a support system while raising kids and working. My husband Jim would often get up to do the 3:00 a.m. feedings and let me sleep longer. He works as hard as I do, and it is the teamwork and respect for each other that counts. We are equal partners in parenthood. We stick together, and we are a united front when it comes to raising our kids. They are teenagers now, and we're in a different phase which is not as physically demanding but more emotionally and financially demanding. High gear parenting means keeping your eyes and ears open and hoping the years of teaching are sinking in.

Recently the phone rang and it was my Dad asking if my son, Bryan, would consider spending his day working in his yard for pay. It was a school holiday and so naturally at 8:30 a.m. the teenagers were still asleep. I told my Dad I would check and have Bryan call him back. I waited until 9:15, woke Bryan up and told him what my Dad wanted. "Oh no, Mom," said Bryan. "I really don't want to do that. I have homework to do, and that's the last thing I want to do." I thought better of what I really wanted to say and said instead, "OK. Call Pop and tell him." Bryan reached for the phone, dialed the number and said, "Hey Pop. You need help today? O.K. sure, yes sir, I will. I will be right over." He hung up, and I kept my mouth shut.

Happiness is having your teenager do the right thing without having to make him. A high gear moment for me.

I think being in high gear means mentally being up to the challenges we face in our careers and finding creative and practical solutions to overcome them. I often tell young women in their 20s without children yet to work hard while they can and use this time to invest in their careers. It's so important to their futures.

CHAPTER 4

Emotions, Emotional Intelligence, and Soft Skills

"Flaming enthusiasm, backed up by horse sense and persistence is the quality that most frequently makes for success."

DALE CARNEGIE

Your emotional intelligence and the strength of your soft skills—friendliness, optimism, team spirit, social graces, language—are critical tools in reaching high gear. We believe women have a competitive edge. We're intuitive, inquisitive, and contemplative. These are advantages in business decision making when you need to rally a client base or management team.

ANNE

When you love what you do, people notice and your enthusiasm becomes contagious. Steve Jobs, Henry Ford, Madame Curie, Romi Haan—these change agents threw themselves into their work. In fact, it was never work to them, it was life.

Romi Haan is South Korea's housewife turned inventor. A hard-driving entrepreneur, she runs a global corporation with revenues in excess of $120 million today.

As the mother of two young sons and with a prestigious career in South Korea's Ministry of Education, she felt she was wasting time cleaning her floors twice a day on her hands and knees. Wasn't there a better way? she thought. She set out to invent a floor cleaner that infused steam and could reduce cleaning time by hours while producing a more sanitized, environmentally kind result.

Three family members, including herself, mortgaged their homes to supply her the capital to bring her idea to market. Did her college degree give her entrée to bank decision makers and product buyers, all of whom were men? No. Did her prior career success shorten her entrepreneurial learning curve? No. It was her passion, determination, and relentless drive to succeed in the face of precipitous odds that induced breakthrough. In essence, it was her soft skills.

In Romi's mind, she was freeing Korean women from a time-consuming household chore and overcoming the "social isolation that went with being a woman in the male-dominated Korean business world." ("When the world says no," *MORE Magazine*, February 2012.)

Emotional intelligence is learning how to read signals, learning when and when not to speak in a meeting, knowing what to say and how to say it, learning how to offer constructive criticism and how to receive it. For a quick glance at a person's self-discipline and emotional intelligence, I look at their social media profiles. If I read a tweet from an individual that says, "Can't wait to be out of this boring meeting. TGIF!" and they clearly state where they work, it's a poor reflection on their emotional intelligence.

If you're reading this book, and you're a young lady in college, I offer encouragement. Don't waste valuable time and precious emotional energy obsessing about maintaining straight As. As a business owner and employer, I am impressed with straight As, and I too worked hard for them in college. But what I am more impressed with is what you've done with your knowledge and the people you've met. Who have you introduced yourself to? Does your University president know who you are? Have you tapped into your professors' lifelong experiences and wisdom? Will they make valuable introductions for you and speak on your behalf? Where are you making a difference?

Focus more on the strength of the connections you're making in school and the power of a well-placed internship. Be able to work well with others on a team. Bring the emotional intelligence, curiosity, and big ideas that business craves.

When you leverage these skills at the negotiating table, you remove the question of *How much money are you asking for?* and replace it with *I need this person in my company; how can we make it work?*

When I started my own business, no client ever asked me what my GPA was. They were hiring my energy, ideas, and ambition. Passion and enthusiasm are palpable, and when I see it in an individual, I make every effort to harness it, hire it, and make a place for it on my team.

AMY

Success and profitability know no gender. As a woman in business, you must control your hormones and save the tears for the drama class. If you expect to be successful in business—especially in a male-dominated world—you must be tough emotionally. And you must admit, right off the bat, that men still run the business world, and we are deluding ourselves if we fight that. So it is important to go ahead and accept this fact with the goal of aiming to work alongside our male counterparts.

Recent studies suggest that men are more comfortable with other male co-workers. Assuming that is true and the cards are stacked against us, that means we have to work and think a bit differently. I have experienced this truth for the past 25 years. I have worked in many organizations—large and small—and in the south, in particular, it is reality. Does that mean we throw in the towel and go home? Some women do, and we should honor that choice. For me throwing in the towel wasn't part of the plan. Instead, I studied how men worked and watched them closely. I played golf (although I don't like it), went to lunches, attended sporting events, and made sure I was visible in their world. I was also careful to be respectful of their positions while simultaneously being strong enough to speak up in the appropriate ways. I knew I was a comfortable sidekick in the office when I could actually interrupt them and get away with it.

Recently a male CEO said, "Amy, I have met very few women who can remain feminine yet who think like a man." What does this mean? Do I take offense to this? What I figured out was that this was his way of complimenting me. I think what he meant was that I relate well to men in business, because I have learned how to communicate effectively with them. I think a better way to say this is that I try to put myself in their shoes and relate to them in meaningful ways.

As a woman business owner with mostly male clients, I am at the table with men—all very successful—COBs, CEOs, CFOs, VPs and when you are around them so much, you begin to think like they do or at least anticipate what they are going to do and say. This is intriguing to me, and I think about it often. I think this theory might be at the root of why the glass ceiling has persisted. I'm not laying any blame or making excuses for this problem. I am just saying that I see this from my experience and perspective. Men are expected to cut to the chase, deal with facts, and deliver strong messages.

Traditionally, however, women were NOT expected to act this same way, and by doing so a woman could be pegged as problematic, aggressive, or the "b" word. I think the lesson here is this: You use your listening skills and intuitive capabilities to emulate how men communicate in the workplace. How they handle employees, where they sit in meetings, how they resolve a conflict, how they interrupt each other—all of these are insights into management styles. If you are fortunate to be asked to the table, you must accept the ground rules the men set. Have you heard the adage, "He who has the gold makes the rules?" Well, the one with the gold is usually male. That really needs to change, and high gear women are part of that change.

I am reminded of a male boss I once had who decided that our meetings would be held standing up instead of sitting down. He read this in some management book and decided it was a good idea. His end goal was to have shorter meetings. One of his female counterparts asked if we could change it and sit down in meetings. His response was, "My meetings, my rules." That is exactly how most men think. So without going into a gender binge, women, if we expect to play in the male-dominated spaces at work, we need to think the way they do to understand how to communicate with them in a way that benefits us. If you walk into an all-male meeting, and you start talking like you would to a roomful of women, you might get some eye-rolling or worse, they tag you as not credible, unimportant, and have discounted your ideas before you even get the chance to state them.

To the young career women: You are going to have to work with a lot of men in your career. Watch them, learn what makes them tick, and you will be fine. We are given the gift of intuition and gut instinct so we should put those skills to work! I am lucky that I have worked with lots of great men. I've also worked with a lot of women, too, and let me tell you some of the men have been easier to please than some of the women. It's not as much about the gender, but the people you find on your journey. Statistics tell us that we have a long road ahead to impact the workforce.

The concentration at the top hasn't shifted appreciably in years. In 2012, only 18 companies of the Fortune 500 had female CEOs— a mere 3.6 percent. Sixteen percent of C-suite executives and Board members are women. Women are approximately 46 percent of the U.S. workforce. Women earn 77 to 81 cents on the dollar compared to our male counterparts. Few of us will have the opportunity to be a Fortune 100 CEO, so we need to develop our own economic realities. And we must have the emotional intelligence, support, and drive to do so.

Women need to support other women in meaningful ways. An example of this is my friend Mary Singer, CCIM, CPM, President of CRG SustainableSolutions in Memphis. She has been responsible for getting the certification process for women-owned businesses in Tennessee by WBENC (Women's Business Enterprise National Council). Certification provides women-owned businesses access to procurement and other opportunities that result in larger companies giving women-owned businesses a piece of the action. These women are getting business—some of it is really big—they could never have had. Mary told me that a woman-owned electrical contracting company got 15 large contracts in one year as a result of being certified. The Fortune 500 want to do more business with women and getting certified is one way for women-owned businesses to score big. For more information visit www.wbenc.org.

One final story about how men think and why having a female perspective around is a great advantage. Five years ago I was in a client meeting where a bet-the-company negotiating session was underway. I was the only woman in the room of 12 men. It was 4 p.m., and we'd been in the meeting since lunch. I could tell the conversation was turning unproductive and everyone was getting fidgety (any mom would have noticed the body language).

While they continued talking, I left and ordered hot tea, coffee, and cookies to be delivered as soon as possible. I interrupted the meeting and said, "I think we could use some sweets and caffeine to give us the energy to wrap this up before dinner."

They were majoring in the minors. The negotiations had come down to something so ridiculously small I felt like they were little boys arguing about who got to ride in the front seat. I wanted to yell, "I call shotgun!" Instead, I fed them. I didn't wait for permission to order food, or let someone else take charge. It's important for women to play to their strengths and take charge when they should.

It was an intuitive gesture based on my experiences as a mother. Women are good at reading signals, interpreting our environments, and staying on task. We should celebrate these abilities. The group was able to quickly close negotiations after our short break.

Women know when a room has lost focus. We know when intelligent conversation snags. It's pretty simple, really. Our gender uniqueness is a strength. I think smart women value smart men, know how to communicate with them, and appreciate that our differences are a powerful combination when played together.

CHAPTER 5

Be Strong, Decisive, and Disciplined

"I knew at a very young age I wanted to run a company, and in school and beyond I was training all my life for what I do today."

DENISE C. MORRISON, CEO, CAMPBELL SOUP COMPANY

ANNE

Not long ago I attended an executive event where a successful businesswoman was introducing herself and an aggressive agenda to a group of 60 business owners, influencers, government leaders, and international CEOs. I admire this leader and her strong commitment to making a difference for her customers and community. She runs a business with seven-figure revenue. She began her opening remarks with a story about her mother's reaction when she told her that a board had appointed her chair.

"They appointed *you*?" her mother said. She laughed as she told it with the warm-hearted intention to inject humor, but in a room full of male business leaders I couldn't help but cringe. No male executive I know would stand in front of a business group and begin with self-deprecating humor.

Women should never position themselves as laughable or as a surprising choice for leadership. If we want to be highly regarded as leaders and capable contributors, don't make it a laughing matter.

The few women who have reached statewide and national leadership roles lead with pride and confidence.

Denise Morrison, CEO of Campbell Soup Company, shares this story in an interview with *The Wall Street Journal*: "In 2007, *The Wall Street Journal* did an article on our family, and they put in that I wanted to be CEO. I remember getting phone calls from people saying, 'I can't believe you said that. What if you don't get it?' And I'm like, 'The thought never crossed my mind.'"

To reach high gear, we should exhibit strength, decisiveness, and self-discipline. We need to be the role models that young women need.

Choose two or three influential female leaders in your community and observe their leadership skills. How do they gain respect? What is their reputation? What boards do they serve on? What initiatives do they lead? What do they write?

There are commonalities among high gear business people. Cultivate relationships with these movers and shakers. It is not hard to notice who's doing brave things in your community. Introduce yourself to them, even if their initiatives are outside your industry. Volunteer for the Strategic Planning Committee of a board. To sit at the table with executives who command respect and create plans for 50 years in the future is a treasure. Stay close by their sides!

A decisive step toward high gear is to look for opportunities to secure a Sponsor. "Sponsors are like mentors, except they advocate for advancement," states Catalyst, a women in business research firm. "Sponsors combine power, influence, and a willingness to promote you—and they have the clout to do something concrete. The results can be dramatic."

A good Sponsor will have seen your work in action—how you collaborate, how you think, the strength of your big ideas. From those first-hand observations, he or she can advise and support your goals as you put your strategy in action. Waiting to be noticed for your hard work and fresh ideas is not an option for high gear. Go big or go home.

The following story is told on a Catalyst.org blog post about Supreme Court Justice Elena Kagan and her powerful Sponsor, Abner J. Mikva:

"Mikva learned the value of sponsorship early on. During his first year of law school, he tried to volunteer with the Democratic Party. 'Who sent you?' asked the man behind the desk of the local party office.

'Nobody,' Mikva replied.

'We don't want nobody nobody sent,' the man huffed."

Find the biggest Somebody that you can connect with and add value to the relationship. You'll both be stronger for it.

Margaret Thatcher, one of the most decisive and influential female leaders of the 20th century, was called the Iron Lady as a disparagement, but she perceived it as a compliment. What traits helped her achieve high gear? She could accept responsibility and have a deeper concern for being respected than for being well liked. Like her friend Ronald Reagan, she was known for "sincere optimism with a deep toughness." The best leaders engender significant respect and support from their employees, not by leading with consensus, but by leading with decisiveness and authority.

"To me consensus seems to be: the process of abandoning all beliefs, principles, values, and policies in search of something in which no one believes, but to which no one objects; the process of avoiding the very issues that have to be solved, merely because you cannot get agreement on the way ahead. What great cause would have been fought and won under the banner 'I stand for consensus'?" Margaret Thatcher (*The Downing Street Years*, p. 167).

AMY

It takes a strong woman to start and run a business, but women are strong by design. If you study history, you can find myriad examples of strong, influential women. Wars were fought over strong women. Women actually have a competitive advantage on many levels.

I think our U.S. corporate world has—to this point—made it almost impossible for women to succeed and balance what they need to balance. That's why being your own boss and starting your own business is an excellent opportunity to shift into high gear. Women CAN do it all. Who says we have to work 8 to 5? If I can bill $3,000 for a half-day of work, that's working smarter and creating value.

Traditionally, service businesses like mine and Anne's bill for time. Time is a non-renewable resource. Don't waste it! We have to use our creativity to see business differently, and for me, to leverage my firm's resources properly and efficiently. I think it is my 25-plus years of experience that allows me to do the most important things first. It's easier to pick low-hanging fruit, but more rewarding to reach higher and pick what's worth more.

Another advantage to building your own business is to be a trailblazer. I hire creative, younger talent who I hope to lead and inspire. I give them the flexibility they need while commanding excellence in client service and management. They know that if they need to take a day off or schedule personal time during the week, I will support that. In turn, they know I expect them to get the work done no matter what day of the week it is.

If you are in PR, you know that the media never sleeps and social media has given us a 24/7 expectation from our clients. As an employer, I see time very differently than traditionally viewed. A few quick tips I have given my team: Don't schedule non-billable meetings during peak billable time. Start your day early by getting at least an hour of production in before you get to the office. Use that quiet time to get important things done. Meet with sales reps after hours. If they really want to sell you something, they'll meet you at

5:30. Use your lunches productively—take a new prospect to lunch or someone you can learn from.

Do high gear tasks first, above all else. We also organize our time well. That means if I have to have client meetings at the other end of town, I schedule several back-to-back to make the most of my time. If you have days when you need a helicopter, you aren't organizing your time well. We have had to learn this the hard way.

The current state of the U.S. economy may force corporations to rethink and reset the workforce and labor pool. As we write this book, *Forbes* magazine has just released an article about the past five years being the worst in American business history since the Great Depression. Very disturbing for some; yet where there are challenges, I see opportunities. As high gear businesses, we must seek new opportunities, challenge traditional roles and rules, and embrace change passionately.

Four years ago, when the real estate market was at its worst in decades, I was paying high rent for class A office space in one of Memphis's swankiest buildings. I was subleasing from a large law firm who decided they were going to raise my rent. When my lease was up, instead of renewing, I decided to do something crazy. I decided to *buy* a commercial space for my firm to use in the heart of Memphis's downtown South Main historic art district.

I found an art gallery occupied by an artist who needed to sell. It was smaller than what I had, but who needs private offices and big conference rooms these days? So, I bought it, restored it, and my note is half of the cost of my lease in the old space. I realized I could pay myself instead of someone else. My payoff on the space I own will take about six more years, and I know for certain what my financial obligation for my space is. I am in control of my real estate decisions, and I don't have a landlord telling me what to pay. Another high gear decision for my business.

Since founding my firm in 1994, I have looked back only to learn and make good decisions about the future. Many of the reasons for my success include aligning with good men who have recognized my abilities and who have championed my cause and, quite frankly, have hired me: Frank Ricks, architect and co-founder of Looney Ricks Kiss; the late Bobby Cox, former founder of law firm Waring Cox and former member of the Board of Directors of FedEx; Walk Jones, architect and former CEO of Walk Jones & Francis Mah architectural firm; Charlie Hill, attorney, former boss, and friend; Mike McManus, long-time client and supporter; Rusty Linkous of Linkous Construction; Bryan Smith of Lexus of Memphis; Mike Starnes, a former CEO who helped me get into leadership groups when I was only in my 20s; and Phil Trenary, friend and former CEO of Pinnacle Airlines and current senior strategist/consultant.

All of these great men believed in me and some are still my clients today. By hiring me, they endorsed me but that had to be earned by being smart and working hard.

Decisive action. My two favorite words. You can't be in public relations and be indecisive. I have had to make quick and accurate decisions, sometimes on the fly. Experience matters. High gear business women are decisive by nature. We don't mess around. One of my favorite terms comes from my husband, a CFO and accomplished businessman. When he's tired of people "messing around" and not making a decision, he says: "Quit fondling the issue." Just get to the bottom line and deal with the facts.

Women in important roles cannot afford to delay or avoid decision-making. It's one of the most important business skill sets one can possess, and it's gender neutral. Some women prefer to build consensus for ideas. This is great when you have the time, and if the right people are involved. However, what I'm talking about is when it's bet-the-company time; you have to make a decision with the best information you have and act.

An example from the trenches: We were deep in a public relations crisis with a client. The lawyers didn't want us to talk to the media at all. I have come to appreciate the legal teams I work with and understand their views, but at this point, I turned to the CEO and said: "There comes a time when you must make a 'bet-the-company' decision. Now is one of them. If we don't talk, everyone else tells our story for us. You must weigh legal versus the court of public perception. What's it going to be?"

He sided with the lawyers. The media ate the company alive. Hindsight ruled. My recommendation was the better strategy, but they didn't use it. You win some, you lose some—but you have to be ready to stand by your guns. Decisive action. Keep those words close to your vest.

CHAPTER 6

Connect the Dots
All the Way to the Top

"You're known by the company you keep."

 AESOP'S FABLES 255

ANNE

To reach high gear, keep self-limiting thoughts and people at bay. When you choose whom to spend time with, seek the brightest, most respected, smartest individuals—male and female. *These are the executives who have the power to advance your ideas, promote your skills, hire your company, and pay for your talent.* Connecting with executive leadership has helped us add influence to our network and tap into the knowledge of some of America's greatest executives. Aim high, be strategic, and give back.

How do you reach out to executives? Simple. You ask. What is the worst that can happen? The person says No. But at least you tried. I believe I do good work. I believe I have much to learn from others. And I believe that executives can learn from women in business.

Beginning in my early days at the publishing house, I learned there will always be the Bettys of the world. Men and women who are satisfied with mediocrity; those who do not wish to push any envelope and certainly do not want to risk failure. A few leaders I want to learn from and work with are Denise Morrison (Campbell Soup CEO); Laura Alber (Williams-Sonoma, Inc. President & CEO);

the women who are members of 85 Broads; and the members of *The Wall Street Journal* Women in the Economy Task Force.

High gear opportunities come in surprising venues. In 2002, my oldest son was recognized at our district's Boy Scouts of America Eagle Scout dinner. At beautiful Founder's Hall in Hershey, Pennsylvania, the evening was extraordinary not only in the quality of young men honored, but in the Who's Who of the business community sitting in the seats.

The keynote for the evening was Derek Hathaway, then-CEO of Harsco, Inc., a Fortune 1000 company. An excellent speaker with a captivating British accent, Derek recounted fondly a story of his youth in England and the first company he ever bought. He told how his elementary teachers did not think he was most likely to succeed. He even held up his elementary school report card with uninspiring comments from his teacher.

I was so impressed with his authenticity and journey that I wrote him a letter the next week and shared my thoughts. Of note is that I was working out of a home office with no prior introduction to him, and he was a CEO with global influence and leadership. He kindly wrote me back and sent me the CD of the evening program. That began a relationship with Derek and his wife Margaret that I still treasure—a global leader who graciously shares insights and wisdom with me. Why? Because I asked. Now retired, he recently hosted a think tank with Ian Bremmer, a world-renown geo-political scientist and author of *G-Zero*.

I was thrilled to be invited to the A-list event and engage in higher-order thinking about economics, world power, and leadership. All because I initiated a high gear relationship years prior. "Nothing ventured, nothing gained" indeed. **Although our book is titled *Women in High Gear*, it by no means implies that women should cultivate an all-female circle of influence or mentors.**

In 2009, I came across a YouTube video titled *A Conversation with Alan Mulally*, the Ford CEO, where he is explaining Ford's

$23.6 billion home improvement loan and how Ford was restructuring without government bailouts. It was genius. I was impressed with his communication skills, his demeanor, his decisiveness, his confidence, and his strategic insights. He spoke directly to the camera and into the hearts of the American public. The video was uploaded on December 1, 2008, and four days later he was documenting Ford's strategy to Congress.

From that day, I have followed Alan Mulally's leadership at Ford and tried to apply his strategies on a micro-level to my business world. Ford stood alone as an independent company during the bailouts and bankruptcies of GM and Chrysler. From CEO at Boeing to CEO at Ford Motor Company, Mulally leads with "confidence, discipline, and a fierce desire to win."

In our digital age, it's extremely easy to find leaders who have shifted into high gear and whom you can learn from. Mulally's management principles of leading with a compelling vision, comprehensive strategy, relentless implementation, all stakeholders on board, and communication to everyone turned Ford around and is equally vital to small business success.

It is an understatement to say that my business strategy and client services have been influenced by this Fortune 10 executive. With sincerity and graciousness, reach out to the best executive role model you know and start listening and learning.

Businesswomen should be comfortable talking to and working with executives in the C-suite. You must believe that you are equal to the task of sharing wisdom, ideas, and give-and-take criticisms. Relationships are key to making the connections you need to reach the top.

Keith Ferrazzi, author of *Who's Got Your Back*, is spot on with his advice: "Those who have a few close, deep relationships are able to get the feedback, perspective, and input that are the lifeblood of effective decision makers. The better you become at building such relationships, the better you'll be at what you do, and the more value you'll bring to the table, whether you work inside or outside an organization."

If high gear is an executive position in your firm, then take on the tasks that others don't want, start initiatives that will grow the bottom line, surround yourself with creative people who think differently. Ideas are the currency of today.

No one reaches high gear as a solo trekker. We surround ourselves with smart, savvy women who are trailblazers. They work in corner offices and daily lift others up. Their spirit and enthusiasm are contagious and their work ethic is performance based. We find them in many different places around the world.

AMY

A client and friend of mine, Judy McLellan, of the legendary residential real estate powerhouse JudyMac Team, works in a mostly female industry. She's the top agent for the Mid-South's leading real estate company, CryeLeike, and has been every year since 1997. When you're a working woman in a female-dominated profession, you always have to be on top of your game. "I will do whatever it takes to accomplish my goals," Judy says often and that determination is what defines high gear. She stresses that you have to differentiate yourself from the pack, be productive, and pay your dues:

> "In real estate, there is only one gear, and it's high. If you stay in low speed, you will never get it done. My advice to younger women starting careers is not to expect a high gear career if you only work 9 to 5.
>
> My high gear career moments have changed both my life and career. When my husband, Mickey McLellan, came to work on the team it changed my business model and allowed me to focus on sales. That really took our business to a new level of growth.

Our business allows you to reach any goal; we don't have constraints in real estate because we are entrepreneurs, and the perspective is different than that of a corporate organization. Any man that is smart enough to get behind a woman can soar and everyone will embrace him. Smart men are those who support women. We need both genders in the workplace.

Another high gear moment was when we invested in branding. Years ago, we paid high prices to develop a brochure and brand our team—it was money well spent. The return on investment has been evident and the decision to brand the 'JudyMac Team' has positively impacted our bottom line. Our leap into Twitter and social media has also changed the way we are perceived. We're accessible in a whole new way and able to show the personality of the team and the individuals that make up that team. When you hire top talent, you want them to shine and social media makes that easier. The Internet has been a game-changer for our team."

Another good friend says, "Women, be curious, be resilient, be strong, have fun but do it in high gear!"

Social media has been a powerful new tool for us to connect with people that we never would have met otherwise. And it's an immediate opportunity to engage and learn from smart, talented business leaders from around the world.

Through Twitter, I have had some amazing experiences and met some powerful people. The key is to follow smart people based on what they share and who they share with. Find executives to champion your cause, but ask yourself in advance what you can do for them. I never ask any C-level for anything unless I have done something significant for him or her.

In 1992, I was the in-house marketing director for one of Memphis's most prestigious real estate firms. The late founder was also a founding member of the Augusta National Golf Club, where the Masters Golf Tournament is played. This man was a personal friend of a former United States President. I was 28. One of my CEO friends knew this gentleman and called me to say: "Amy, one of my lifelong dreams is to play golf at Augusta National, and if you can introduce me to your boss, I will volunteer my jet to fly everyone there and back as many times as they want."

WOW! Now this is what I would call a high gear request. I proceeded to set up a power meeting between these parties which went fabulously. I was able to connect the dots, and the two parties became close friends and did business together afterwards. Golf and private jets were involved.

The CEO told me that I had helped him achieve the biggest of his goals and for that he'd always be grateful. As a result, I had access to this CEO when and if I needed it. Women in high gear don't keep score, but they do know that helping people reach their goals comes full circle. When my name was floated for a coveted position, I learned that this CEO put a good word in on my behalf. That is what being in high gear is about. The ability and knowledge to connect the dots.

Not long ago, I wrote a blog post about how FedEx, headquartered in my hometown of Memphis, responded to a packaging crisis with positive social media engagement. The CEO of FedEx, whom I have met but don't know well, came into a restaurant where I was dining. He and I had a brief exchange, and as we talked, I realized the entire restaurant was focused on him, perhaps wondering why he was talking to me.

Here I was sitting in a restaurant talking to the CEO of FedEx. That's high gear y'all.

Further connecting and thinking fast, I told him that I had been the speaker at his digital team's social media meeting. As he left the table, he turned and said, "Now please tell me you are working for us at FedEx?" I smiled and said, "No sir, not yet." He asked me to email him. I did, and he answered me back personally. Another high gear highlight for me in my career.

One of my networking principles is that I always try to do for others what they do all the time. Simple gestures like paying for an executive's lunch or sending a bottle of wine to their table are symbols of creative relationship-building. That's how I connect the dots. For more on social media dot connecting, I highly recommend my dear friend Mark Schaefer's book, *Return on Influence*, where he delves deep into the power of online influence.

CHAPTER 7

Build Your Personal Brand: Tell Your Story

"Don't bunt. Aim out of the ballpark.
Aim for the company of immortals."

DAVID OGILVY

ANNE

If you don't believe in yourself, don't expect others to carry your PR banner for you. Humility has its place in business and leadership, but if Google defines who we are, then it's incumbent on us to pipe the web with client successes and business accomplishments.

Women tend to soften accomplishments or return compliments with, "Oh, you do great work too!" Instead of saying, "Thank you for noticing." If no one knows who you are, or the high quality of your work, it's not a business advantage, and it's certainly not profitable.

Former U.S. Secretary of State Madeleine Albright didn't enter the workforce full time until she was 40. "I learned to speak up and interrupt," she said to *The Wall Street Journal* Women in the Economy.

To reach high gear, be artful in building your professional and personal brand. Initiate programs, fill needs, connect with editors and editorial boards. Apply for and be strategic about winning Best Women in Business, Forty Under 40, and the Athena Awards. Go to conferences in New York City, at NASDAQ, in Los Angeles, Orlando, or Chicago.

Broaden your circle of influence. A good first step is to start in your own backyard. If your chamber of commerce or women in business groups don't know that you can hit it out of the park, then start building your brand. Each time your successes are highlighted and accomplishments noted, it's a plus for your company and a good example to young women and men following in your footsteps.

A core service that we offer is Executive Positioning. I call it Executive Storytelling. Whether it's on a TV commercial, a YouTube video, or throughout an opinion editorial, people remember stories more than they do data. Almost every CEO that we work with has been concerned with the balance of confidence and the danger of appearing narcissistic. I challenge all of them to look at the situation from another point of view. What advantage is it in business, if you succeed, lead a company from loss to profit, or win an award for character and community service and no one knows about it?

For example, Richard E. Jordan II, CEO of Smith Land & Improvement Corporation, has been leading a $70 million company for more than two decades. In spite of Harrisburg, Pennsylvania's dour financial outlook, Rick is widely recognized as a positive voice of "Ground Truth." In his tweets, Facebook posts, blog posts, YouTube videos, meetings, and panel presentations, he sends a strong message that business is healthy and that central Pennsylvania's economy and workforce remain competitive.

I admire business leaders who remove the veil of secrecy to tell their stories in biographies, speeches, and documentaries. How will the next generation of men and women learn to lead? These organic experiences are rarely learned in classrooms unless there's an executive teaching. The ripple effect of first-person stories is powerful and relates directly to small business bottom lines. And that's one of the biggest goals Amy and I have for our book—to show others how we are reaching high gear and how you can too.

Organizations struggle with branding as well. I serve on the board of The Salvation Army Greater Harrisburg, and when I was asked to join, I told our Advisory Board Chair that I had no idea they delivered so many services to those in need. Being the best kept secret in town does not produce a revenue stream nor help gain publicity—both critical elements to a sustaining organization. Part of my role on the board is to make sure we tell our story so businesses can donate time and resources. "Doing the Most Good" should have a sister tagline of "And Go Tell It on the Mountain!"

I spend significant time cultivating relationships with the media—print, TV, radio, and digital. I want to be known as the Go-To person for a great story and dependable, fact-checked information. Many of our local media have told me they follow me on Twitter and Facebook to find potential story ideas and sources.

During Hurricane Sandy, two reporters at WHTM ABC TV 27 created a regional Twitter hashtag (#SandyCenPa) that several of us used to share up-to-the-minute news to keep our region safe. The Governor, utility companies, the Pennsylvania National Guard, the media, hospitals, county emergency preparedness directors, and many others joined in. Because of the volume of safety news we were sharing, the Deeter Gallaher Group was recognized as an authority and as a reliable source of news.

Monitoring the hurricane on Twitter from across the pond was the BBC who reached out to me on Twitter to discuss our hashtag and its potential to save lives and direct people to safety. After several direct messages, they called me for a live interview on how we were harnessing the power of social media in an emergency. This proved to be serious brand-building cachet. Each time I create timely and helpful business information, it reinforces the strength of my personal and business brand.

At *The Wall Street Journal's* Women in the Economy event, 120 women gathered to chart a course forward and capitalize on women's economic power. One of our Task Force outcomes was to encourage more women entrepreneurs to tell their stories on the opinion pages of national and international news media

(See Chapter 11). Again, how can women follow in our steps if we're shy about telling our story?

AMY

You are now who Google, Facebook, Twitter, and YouTube say you are. While technology and social media have been game changers, the old saying that "perceptions are reality" is still true. Social media makes it all happen with immediacy. We used to think public relations pitches were limited to print and TV. Now, you can tweet a news bite, and your story can go viral. I have been quoted as saying, "You are what you tweet" and "Twitter is the tripwire for news." In this digital age where we work at the speed of thought, both are powerful and well-supported statements.

On every channel, tell your story or someone else will. If you aren't creating your digital footprint with blogs, tweets, and videos, who will know you? If you are a target for an acquisition and you have no footprint, and no story, are you influential and valuable? If you have a crisis and have no digital presence or history of what you believe or what your culture promotes, do you have an advantage? NO. If you have no strong story online, you are at the mercy of the media. Public relations and personal branding begin with you.

How important is it to tell your story first? Our firm was simultaneously representing a real estate company and a large corporate client. The corporate client was scouting a new headquarters location—big news indeed. The media had caught on that something was happening, and we were scrambling to close the real estate deal before someone leaked it to the press. Too many people knew about the deal. It would only be a matter of time before a reporter had some version of the story.

Knowing we couldn't afford a leak to the press, I convinced the lawyers to distribute non-disclosures to everyone who had intel about the deal underway. When you have important news like this, it is essential to manage the story. We were able to keep a tight lid on it and worked with the reporter to get the story written and published on our timeframe and based on facts once the transaction was complete.

Another story didn't go so well, but thankfully it was not my client. I was at a chamber of commerce luncheon where a big announcement was to have been made about a recent corporate relocation. Somehow the story was leaked, and it ran in the news the day before the luncheon. When the CEO of the company coming to our city got up to the microphone, he said, "This news got here before we did." It was a gentle way of telling everyone that the story got away from them. Lessons are often learned the hard way. When you have breaking news pending, use non-disclosures and insist the legal team be on board with you in this process.

CHAPTER 8
Emotional Resilience

"Your time is limited, so don't waste it living someone else's life. Don't be trapped by dogma—which is living with the results of other people's thinking. Don't let the noise of other's opinions drown out your own inner voice. And most important, have the courage to follow your heart and intuition. They somehow already know what you truly want to become. Everything else is secondary."

STEVE JOBS

ANNE

Emotional resilience: You won't go far without it. It is, perhaps, the most important trait you'll need to succeed and achieve as a woman in high gear. If you want to succeed and bring tremendous value to the table, be memorable, be known for "Getting things done," and develop a thick skin.

When I visited Alan Mulally's office at Ford World Headquarters in Dearborn, Michigan, he gave me what I call the Ford Creed. He wrote it. It is a small, plastic pocket card that every Ford employee has—all 244,000 in 90 plants around the world. What caught my eye was one of the bullet points. An expectation so important that it made it to the card—Emotional Resilience.

"Have a can do, find a way attitude and emotional resilience."

Ever since I read the card, I have tried to put the principle into practice for every business experience, including at the board tables I sit on. I have become an apostle.

Building a thick skin takes conscious effort and a determination to focus on the power of working together—to understand our potential en masse.

To help me keep an exterior like the Honey Badger, I ask myself the following five questions:

1. **Do I have to be perfect?**
2. **Do I have to be right?**
3. **Do I have to be in command?**
4. **Do I have to be the focus of attention?**
5. **Do I have to be liked?**

I confess I struggle with these. If like me, you answered Yes to any (or all!) of these, you need to focus on another critical component of high gear: self-awareness. Know Thyself, attributed to Socrates, is a characteristic mastered by successful leaders. They know their skills, they know their weaknesses. They know who to get on their bus, they see the end zone, they don't get in the way of forward momentum, and they're secure with themselves. **They know how it feels not to be liked, and they're over it.**

How we respond to challenges, crises, public criticisms, and office backbiting defines us. What emotions are you portraying? What responses are you invoking?

An important aspect of emotional resilience is remembering why we need it. If you own your own company, you will undoubtedly experience a client who does not pay. Hopefully, it will be rare, but it will happen. In the service business where you are selling ideas or intangibles, it's not uncommon for a client to feel she didn't receive what was promised, or didn't benefit from the outcome delivered.

In high gear, you cannot take your eye off the profitability of your company or your department. There are instances where to prove being right demands too much time and energy and is actually preventing you from focusing on being profitable in your core business.

For example, a firm was referred to us by another client. After several months of positive work and experiences, things began to fall apart. Invoices weren't paid, and thousands of dollars in service were already invested. Our work for them was showing up on Google. An interview feature with a magazine had even been brokered. Meanwhile, the client declared they were not going to pay the outstanding invoices.

The amount of emotional energy required to resolve the situation was enormous. Lengthy email threads, voicemail messages, apologies for misunderstandings, and finally an appointment with my attorney. At the end of an hour of document sharing and explanations, my attorney said, "Anne, don't ever lose sight of your wallet."

Both of my brothers, who are mentors to me and business owners, challenged me during this experience with: "Do you have to be right? This is the cost of doing business. Get over it and move on. Get paid what you can and mark it off to experience."

What did I learn? I was too emotionally invested and had zero resilience. I lost sleep; I spent too much time with hypotheticals and brooding over unfairness. The greatest damage was not the loss of revenue, but the loss of creative time that could have been spent strategizing over new ideas for great clients. Instead, my skin was thin, and I was resentful, mad, offended, hurt, and insistent that I was right.

High gear women do not take their eyes off the bottom line. They ask: "What's the cost?" In *The Art of War for Women*, author chin-ning chu reminds us that the nature of war is the battle of money. "It takes a lot of money to fight a battle. Running a company also takes a lot of money. If you are hoping to advance within your organization, you must keep that point in mind. On your desk, in addition to the picture of your kids, lover, or husband, place a picture of your whole department—maybe even a photo that shows your entire company. You are working for them as well."

AMY

Emotional resilience reminds me of my kids. Kids have that ability to bounce back. Like Teflon, nothing seems to penetrate their resilient personalities (and I'm talking about simple stuff here—no drama or trauma). In boardrooms teeming with testosterone, as a woman, you simply must be resilient. You must be impervious to derogatory or degrading comments, and you must fight to keep your emotions intact. You must have a childlike ability to bounce back. And that means forgetting fast and moving forward. Kids get punished or reprimanded for what they do one minute, and then the next minute they are running out the door singing—at least this is so of my kids. They don't pout or dwell on the negative or the past.

This is a great way to look at being resilient in the workplace, and something I only noticed after having kids. I think we can learn great lessons from the very young! They are passionate and unaffected by attention. That is another trait we can take to the office. Sometimes younger women especially become so focused on being in the center of attention that they forget the client is the center of attention.

High gear women get the job done first. If praise comes along with it, that's a bonus. I'm sure Anne and I could write another book about the times we've been the ones getting it done while others get the credit. The important thing here is that you know you did it. High gear women use that to add to their confidence levels. And being passed over in the praise department makes you stronger and more resilient.

In my case, I used my wins to launch my business. I was working hard for others with no path to ownership or partnership. I was in my fourth year of working for a law firm (this was my third job), and unless you were a lawyer, ownership in the firm was off the table. I was doing my job so well that when I realized nobody appreciated it besides me, it was time to take the leap. I will never forget walking into Bobby Cox's office at Memphis's oldest and arguably most powerful law firm. Mr. Cox was then the Secretary of the Board of Directors of FedEx and a long-time friend to its founder, Mr. Frederick W. Smith.

I knocked on his door, and he yelled at me in his gruff, ex-military style voice, "What? Come in!" He was the ruler, and his door needed a disclaimer on it, I promise you. I opened the door and when he finally looked up from what he was doing, he gave me permission to enter. I did, but did not sit down, as I had no intention of staying very long.

"Sir, I would like for you to be the first to know that I'm starting my own marketing firm immediately, and I'd like to have your firm as my only law firm client," I said. I might as well have told him I was the Queen of England by the way he looked at me.

"Like hell you are! You are not doing that," he said. I took a deep breath and replied, "Well, then, I quit. I was hoping you would embrace my entrepreneurial spirit; I can see that you are being your stubborn old self." I was trying to joke him into reality and convince him that I was serious. He smiled a little—which was big—and said, "Oh, hell, OK. What do you need and sit down, dammit. I don't have all day!" This was vintage Bobby.

My emotional resilience paid off. With my law firm's support, I started my business and retained them as my first client. Sadly, Robert L. Cox lost his long battle with cancer and passed away just after 9/11—one of the saddest times in my life. A week after our pow wow in his office, he wrote me a letter on old-fashioned, engraved letterhead congratulating, supporting, and calling me "one of his favorite people ever." I cherish that letter and look at it often. It was an amazing high gear moment in my career.

How do you exhibit emotional resilience? Here are nine tips that have served me well.

1. Hold your tongue. Silence is best at times.
2. Take notes. When things get heated, it's a great diversion. When things aren't going my way, I defer to note taking as a strategic tactic. People running the meetings have said, "Um, Amy, are you working on something else?" I say, "Oh, no, I'm just documenting." That gets them thinking!
3. Know when to walk away. This requires experience.
4. Trust your gut. A rat is a rat.
5. Always do the right thing, even if it costs you money.
6. Never let them see you sweat. I've excused myself from meetings with "Oh my, a client has a PR crisis, and I must go now." Creating a diversion or a crisis can be very productive. As Gini Dietrich (@GiniDietrich), author of the blog *Spin Sucks*, said at our Social Slam conference in 2011, "Sometimes you have to create your own crisis in order to get something done." I love this strategy.
7. Charge more for high maintenance clients. These are the ones who want to know what you've done for them today and the ones who call your cell after you just left a meeting with them.
8. Laugh and make sure you make time for fun, girlfriends, and travel! And of course your spouse too. Sometimes we get so wrapped up in work that we forget it will all be there tomorrow. It's ok to take a break!
9. Say NO. I am in the privileged position to be selective about my clients. I'm saying No to people who don't get it and would tend to abuse my talents and my team.

When you are young in your work journey, you are clearly the most vulnerable. To the 20-year-olds, a word of caution: Assume you know nothing. Don't try to exert your wisdom if you don't have it. You must earn your place by working hard and self-study. If you try and push, you'll get the push back you are looking for. If you do, be ready.

To the 30-year-olds with some experience: tread lightly; your best weapons are accuracy and facts. To the 40-year-old career women: welcome to the kingdom. You have built a career and have worked hard to get there. As I approach my next decade, I hope to spend time coaching others and teaching our young professionals how to shift into high gear.

CHAPTER 9
Social Media, Superconnectors, and High Gear

"To any CEO who's skeptical at all: You have to. You have to create a social enterprise today. You have to be totally connected to everyone who touches your brand. If you don't do that, I don't know what your business model is in five years."

ANGELA AHRENDTS, CEO, BURBERRY

ANNE

High gear women leverage their digital connections and are strategic in connecting the dots. When I joined Twitter on February 24, 2009, (within hours of when Amy joined!), I wanted to add it to our strategic communications efforts and make sure my presence would benefit the business brand. By using Twitter's Search capacity and joining in several Twitter chats, I have amassed a virtual agency of friends and influencers. Regardless of their Klout scores, the real power of influence is that we can pick up the phone and call each other 24/7 should we need advice, services, wisdom, connections, or help in a crisis—all ahead of a news cycle.

It's important to note that Twitter is an access point for high achievers, but the full benefit of a high gear connection is realized when you take the online engagement to an offline relationship.

71

Our Twitter connection took a career high gear when Amy and Glen Gilmore joined me for a leadership event I created with the help of client and event sponsor Richard E. Jordan II, CEO of L.B. Smith Ford Lincoln Inc. and Smith Land & Improvement Corporation. One of my earliest connections on Twitter was Scott Monty (@ScottMonty), Ford's Global Digital Communications Director. His social media leadership and tactical examples have influenced almost every CMO on the planet.

I have reached out to him numerous times for information, hosted him in 2009 for an International Association of Business Communicators event in Harrisburg, and he was instrumental in making my introduction to Alan Mulally. I can honestly say that my social media adoption would not have been as comprehensive or so successful for my clients without the friendship and role model of Scott.

How can you integrate your social media friends with your media friends? Those connections lead to superconnections. When we honored Alan Mulally, part of my strategic communications plan was to have 26 Twitter influencers in the room sharing real-time information and pictures as Mr. Mulally spoke. Amy calls it power tweeting. We had TV, print, and video capturing the event, but Amy, Glen Gilmore, Kathy Snavely, Sherry Christian, Scott Heintzelman, Deb Pierson, Richard E. Jordan II, Marisa Corser, and many others (with Scott Monty tweeting from Dearborn) created a ripple effect in real time by live-tweeting.

The power of this integrated media strategy catapulted my firm into another high gear and netted a new client that evening. The next morning, the president of a global engineering firm called my office and said, "We need your level of social media skills for our firm. When can we start?"

@MarkRaganCEO In the PR and communications world, no one is more learned, experienced, and genuine than Mark Ragan of Ragan Communications. Both Amy and I connected with Mark on Twitter, and he invited us to one of his corporate events hosted at NASDAQ on April 8, 2011, in the heart of Times Square. After a social media-packed day with 100 professional communicators, we closed the markets and watched our picture on the world's highest outdoor digital sign—the NASDAQ MarketSite Tower—all from a Twitter introduction! On our train ride back to Pennsylvania, the idea for this book was born.

@DebWeinstein Deb is a PR mogul in Toronto, and we all met through Twitter in 2010, then in real life at Amy's #BroganMemphis event. Her agency success and ability to leverage the power of traditional and digital tools have positioned Deb as an international resource. We have gathered at conferences and presented on panels together. Deb's generous social media spirit has introduced many people to the new power of strategic public relations.

@2morrowknight Sean Gardner is a renowned blogger from the State of Washington who writes for *The Huffington Post*. Both Amy and I were fortunate enough to be included in his *Huffington Post* article titled "16 Brilliant Business Minds on Twitter." I appreciate Sean's immense knowledge of social media platforms and the people who use them, and have enjoyed long business conversations with him via phone. The company we keep has proven to be business-changing and has certainly raised our social influence. Like Sean, I try to always focus on sharing highly valuable content with a helpful spirit and with the intent to give back.

@AdamsConsulting After Diana Adams and Amy forged a Twitter relationship, they created a fun list of the "75 Badass Women of Twitter." What started as a simple idea has transformed into a brand of its own with tweets, videos, chats, and a Facebook page. Many of us have included #BA75 in our social media profiles and this recognition has become a measure of influence as well. These 75 women are extremely well-connected, and I admire their business acumen and brand building. I was very honored to be included in the group.

@JohnsonWhitney As a prime mover for women living their dreams, Whitney is a business owner, *Harvard Business Review* blogger, and author of *Dare, Dream, Do*. I also met Whitney on Twitter and have sought her counsel on executive education and conferences. When Whitney learned more about my on-ramping story, she introduced me via Twitter to Carol Fisher Cohen, founder of @iRelaunch. Carol asked me to share my story, and she posted it on the iRelaunch website and Yahoo.com. I first heard about 85 Broads from Carol and follow both of these smart women daily to watch where they lead.

There are hundreds of people on the social channels that I continue to learn from, and they enrich my business education. There's no magic bullet to connections and superconnections, but the same rules of communication at work and relationship-building apply online as well. When you reach out and share news and experiences with others, you'll be surprised at the high gear outcomes.

AMY

It's difficult to reach high gear by working under the radar or practicing humble public relations. Creating your personal brand and building credibility is infinitely easier, and more dangerous, in our world of social media. Anne and I both value social media and have benefited greatly from the people we have met, particularly on Twitter. Twitter is one of the best social media platforms for businesses. It is public, global, and simple.

I joined Twitter on February 23, 2009, and I guessed, correctly, that Twitter would grow in popularity and that the reset button for PR had forever changed. Schooled in the traditional PR and communications ways of the 80s and 90s, I know that Twitter is a tool for getting factual information and business links. Our good friend Mark Schaefer's first book titled *The Tao of Twitter* has been widely used in business, and I recommend it as an excellent primer. Little did I know that Twitter would become the superconnector for my business.

As an extension to our belief that you're known by the company you keep, the quickest way to discern the quality and caliber of one's "gear" is to check out their digital tattoo. Who are you tweeting to and what does your content say about you?

There are amazing, powerful, successful, inspirational, educational connections online. Leverage these relationships. How? Pick up the phone.

These are some of our superconnectors: men and women who have helped us change our business models and grow into high gear.

@GlenGilmore I will never forget calling Glen Gilmore, a man I had never met but wanted to based on his Twitter presence and the content he shared. Now he is my legal advisor for social media for my clients and an integral part of my team. He and I have worked together for over two years on social media policy for my clients. He is finishing a new book, *Social Media Law for Business: A Practical Guide for Using Facebook, Twitter, Google+, and Blogs Without Stepping on Legal Landmines* for McGraw-Hill, to be published in 2013. He has also become a dear friend and has been to our home and with our family on several occasions. He is a crisis media expert and one I call on when I need some backup. Little did I realize in 2009 that I had met one of my most important resources through Twitter.

@MarkWSchaefer I also met Mark on Twitter. He outlines how we met in his first book (*The Tao of Twitter*) but basically I read his blog, tweeted with him, and he talked back. When business took me to Knoxville three years ago, I called him in advance and told him I was coming and wanted to meet him. You'll have to read the rest in his book, but since that meeting, we also have collaborated, started Social Slam—one of the most successful social media conferences for business in the country, held in Knoxville each spring (www.soslam.com). I am honored to say I have been a speaker and am the emcee in 2013! And, Mark has written about me, as well as the great connections we have made, in both of his books. How great is that? And, no, he is not paying me. In fact, I wasn't sure I was going to be in either of his books until I saw them for myself. How valuable is it to me as a business owner for a leading author and blogger to refer to me as a "Super Connector"? (See page 17 of *Return on Influence*). What a huge honor for me, and what a great man to know.

@JessicaNorthey Founder of #CMchat (Country Music Chat on Twitter), Jessica is a force! Her chat has generated more than 1.5 billion impressions—and growing—since it began in May of 2011. Jessica hosts this chat every Monday evening with a guest country musician, and it is one of the best on Twitter. She has advanced into live Google+ hangouts and video chats as well. When the Academy of Country Music called inviting her to live-tweet the event in Las Vegas last year, she asked me to join her. We were treated like the mainstream media covering the event and had access to the pressroom where all the award recipients talked individually to the press. It was a once-in-a-lifetime opportunity for me as a PR person from Memphis, TN.

The common thread here is **engagement**. These are just a few of the people in our social media brain trust. They are all critical to our high gear journey and help us stay focused, energized, and tech savvy.

CHAPTER 10

Success Is in the Numbers: Understanding the Bottom Line

*"When I hear prognosticators say,
'Wait until the economy rebounds,' I remind
my people that we ARE the economy."*

PATTI HUSIC, CEO, CENTRIC BANK AND
2013 CHAIR OF THE PENNSYLVANIA BANKERS ASSOCIATION

ANNE

The measurement of high gear success for business owners and executives is in the numbers. High gear individuals understand the story behind the numbers.

The good news is that women-owned businesses are going strong in the U.S. According to the State of Women-Owned Businesses Report for 2012, "there are over 8.3 million women-owned businesses in the United States; 8,345,600 to be precise. As of this year, women-owned firms are generating $1,291,267,100,000 (nearly $1.3 trillion) in revenues and employing 7,697,000 people." That's the power of women in the economy.

Further, "between 1997 and 2012, when the number of businesses in the United States increased by 37 percent, the number of women-owned firms increased by 54 percent—a rate 1½ times the national average."

Common among entrepreneurs is to focus on selling your big idea and gathering a groundswell of support for your concept, and then to map out a business plan to show friends and your banker. As a new business owner puts her house in order, she may underestimate the costs of doing business—everything from the marketing materials, the digital investment, the commercial infrastructure, and the IT services. Thousands of dollars are required up front before one dime of time or product is ever sold.

I was in a business group once where a new business owner shared that he had won a statewide business plan competition. But as the session progressed, I learned that the business was not profitable and was piling up debt. How could that be? How can you win an award for the strength of your business model and ultimately not be a viable business? You have to get the numbers right.

A first-time business owner opened a high-end retail store a few years ago. It was a great concept, but she probably underestimated the costs of bringing an inventory-based business to market. The location was perfect, the story was memorable, the product was desired, the high-end customers bought the product.

She enjoyed early success, but then she diversified—too quickly. She added more high-end inventory. She expanded her space. She went on buying trips and hired a few young ladies to help run the store. With children, it was a lot to juggle.

Sometimes she had to close the store to take care of other responsibilities. It was difficult to give the store the attention a small business requires. But the most important lesson I observed was that she was operating the business as if it were a hobby. When this happens, it can be an expensive lesson in profit and loss.

When I was working from my home office, I was the Jane of all Trades—writer, marketer, CEO, IT expert, invoicer, subcontractor, RFP-er, secretary, coffee brewer, director of first impressions. As I expanded, I had to take a deeper dive into my financials. My commercial landlord wanted all kinds of paperwork and guarantees when I signed my three-year lease. Out of my own naïveté, I was offended that they wanted three years of tax returns and personal guarantees. But that meant that I really needed the wisdom, experience, and a strong relationship with a good banker.

One of my longtime clients is a community bank. I connected with the female CEO years ago and deeply admire her high gear. I continue to learn from Centric Bank CEO Patti Husic who has forged an amazing path in a male-dominated industry. Her leadership skills have opened opportunities on state and national platforms. In 2013, she will be the Chair of the Pennsylvania Bankers Association—only the third female in the organization's 118-year history.

She loves numbers, accountability, big ideas, and getting things done. Her success has earned her recognition as one of *American Banker's* 25 Women to Watch in the U.S., and Centric Bank was featured in a *Wall Street Journal* article for its 30 percent increase in lending. She is always looking for new ways to advance young people and women in her industry and is a champion for small business.

Early on, Patti extolled the necessities of having a solid business foundation. "You have to focus on three building blocks, Anne. You need a good attorney, a good CPA, and a good banker." Such wise words. I had the perfect banker.

When I applied for an executive line of credit, I realized that I should apply for the largest amount my credit history would allow. Patti walked me through the entire process—it's very rare to have the bank CEO journey with you—but she knew how important it was for me to get the numbers right. Banks are in the business of risk, but they're only going to invest with businesses that they believe have the DNA to succeed.

As a purchaser of my services, Patti understood my work ethic and self-discipline. She ran the bank from an entrepreneur's vision, and she understood my deep desire to succeed. I remain grateful for her insights as I have shifted into several more high gears since then.

WOMEN IN HIGH GEAR

I just recently asked her about commercial real estate loan potential, should I find a property in Nashville to purchase. "We'd be glad to help you grow in Nashville, Anne," she said.

If your skill set is not in the numbers, make sure you have a smart CPA who knows small business. You need to keep a keen eye on all financial transactions—from phone bills to office furniture to web hosting fees—and understand that you can't delegate financial responsibility. My CPA is a smart, young entrepreneur who keeps me updated weekly on my finances, and most importantly, I trust him.

I asked my personal board of advisors for recommendations on an attorney and was given a great referral. I remember sitting in the attorney's office, on the 12th floor of their impressive Harrisburg building, thinking I was really out of my league.

"Am I too small for your level of services?" I asked sheepishly. "I'll take care of you, Anne. There are certain things you can't afford to get wrong at this stage," my attorney said. I was so grateful for that advice.

Doing your business and running your business are two different animals. With the right connections and relationships, you'll succeed at both.

AMY

To understand the bottom line, volunteer for projects and positions that involve the numbers. Do you know how your organization makes money? Do you know the difference between revenue and profit?

One of my favorite bankers in Memphis, Dana Burkett, said: "Amy, revenue is ego. Profit is your success marker." Dana is a woman in high gear and one of my Go-To finance minds. An organization can generate revenue, but if they aren't watching profitability, they may not succeed.

Another client, a national public accounting firm, CBIZ, offers a program for their female employees called CBIZ Women's Advantage

(CWA). It directs the development of women professionals through focused leadership, mentoring, and networking programs. My firm has the distinct honor of helping CBIZ bring this national platform and its resources to local Memphis business women in high gear. Women gain access to seasoned professionals who can offer guidance and help them find success in business.

We have launched two important projects through this program: 1. CBIZ has secured the sponsorship of the *Memphis Business Journal*'s "Super Women" business awards program, and 2. We have started regular round table lunch meetings that give 15 women the opportunity to share their business stories. This has become a powerful and profitable program for the firm, as some of these women have gone on to hire my client. Having a network is a good thing; profiting from your network is a great thing. Through this program we are promoting women in business and helping introduce them to other businesses who need them and can hire them.

The National Leader of CWA, Nancy Mellard, feels that her work with CBIZ Women's Advantage has reinforced the value of women's programs. "Companies strive for different results — better employee engagement, advancement of women, more diversity in the C-suite — but so often many of these companies fail to change how they have always done business," Nancy said.

With more women entering the accounting field, this is a great initiative and one that will help women succeed and enter the C-suite in these line or key financial roles. I'm not implying that women in other fields cannot reach the C-suite, but data shows a pattern from line to executive suite.

It is also important here to say to the women who have made it to the C-suite or other high perches: help out a sister when you can! Women must be champions for other women in business assuming these women are capable and credible. I have already said that it is not as much about gender but people. However, when successful women look for ways to help other women climbing the career ladder, that is important. Recently I read an article in *The Wall Street Journal* about the "Queen Bee" syndrome where top women have actually done the opposite, blocking younger women from advancing as if there is not enough room for more women in the hive. This is a terrible trend. Women who intentionally thwart potential in others—male or female—are not high gear.

Another important point in reaching success is that you don't have to be good with finance to recognize that you need to hire someone who is. I chose communications and marketing because they are my strongest skill sets. However, I know that running a business requires an appreciation and understanding of finance, so I have an accounting firm handle my firm's finances.

My CPA, Matt Patrick, acts as my CFO. I consult his professional opinion on hiring, promoting, capital expenditures, and taxes. Make sure you seek a CPA who works with similar businesses and get referrals and recommendations.

I'm better doing what I do best—public relations—so I hire others to do what they do best, when needed. Believing that you are good at everything is not a high gear mentality.

CHAPTER 11

The Power of Communications: "Whoever Tells the Story, Writes History"

"Our starting goal is to increase the number of women thought leaders contributing to key commentary forums—which feed all other media, and drive thought leadership across all industries— to a tipping point. We envision a world in which the best ideas—regardless of where or whom they come from—will have a chance to be heard and shape society and the world."

THE OP-ED PROJECT

ANNE

Your words are the building blocks for your business and personal brand. Although we spend hours each week sharing and retaining information in social media conversations for ourselves and our clients, every PR and marketing strategy begins with carefully chosen words. An important and powerful communication tool for informing, influencing, persuading, and challenging is the opinion editorial.

Early in my business career, I began taking advantage of this incredibly valuable print and digital "real estate." Many people read the editorial pages first, and the remaining news content at leisure. When you are featured on the editorial page voicing your own opinion, it's 800 words from your lens. Far more potent than a source quote, the op-ed can be the foundation for your next high gear ascension. Begin with a topic that you're passionate about, and start to build your reputation and use the currency of your big ideas.

One of the first op-eds I wrote for our Harrisburg newspaper, *The Patriot-News*, was titled "Wrestling mat is training ground for entrepreneurial qualities." As the mother of three sons who wrestled, I observed that entrepreneurs and wrestlers share many of the same traits. Do op-eds have staying power? Just this week, a friend and Penn State University wrestling scholarship sponsor called me to ask if she could send my 2005 op-ed on to Cael Sanderson, Olympic wrestling champion and coach of Penn State's wrestling program, for his campaign to save wrestling in the Olympic Games.

I have since written op-eds on women in the economy and women on boards, the power of the purse, leadership, and many other topics. For excellent guidance on the process of getting published on the opinion pages, visit www.theopedproject.org. You'll also find a weekly tally of the biggest newspapers in the U.S. and what percentage of women versus men appear on the opinion pages. If we hope to increase our influence and numbers in the C-suites and at decision-making tables, op-ed writing should be a powerful tool in our toolkit. It's time to tell our stories.

After your op-ed is published, then leverage the ink into a blog post, a video, a news release, an event, or even a TEDx presentation to reach your next level.

AMY

Anne and I both have had the honor and earned the privilege of being published, serving as a media source, writing op-eds, and speaking to groups on the power of influence and new media. Crafting influential messages that help you and others do more and better business, and using your writing and speaking skills will advance your career, your company, and you as an individual.

My dad keeps a paper file on everything I have ever written—published or not. I'm afraid to go through it, but it is huge. I was prolific in college as an English major and have always had a passion for writing and communicating. Good communication skills and the ability to influence people are critical when owning your business or succeeding in your career.

You must write concise, clear, and factual memos, articles, stories, and books. You must master grammar and punctuation, or find a good editor who can. You must think strategically about word use, especially in the viral age of social media. Every word matters. You are what you tweet!

Social media has given all business a big stage. Combined with being published in newspapers and business magazines, social content creates great Google juice. The ability to be found online is marketing gold. Hubspot coined this "inbound marketing." In the old days, you had to push your story out and hope someone would listen. Today, it's about being discovered on the Internet. Usually, this is good. Beware, however, of the viral nature of posting.

I will never forget a blog post I wrote two years ago about my opinion that Twitter would kill Google+. I wrote it at night (when many bloggers are up working), posted it, and thought little of my words. After all, I wasn't a techie, so why would anyone listen to me? I wasn't writing to the tech audience. I was blogging to my clients, right? BIG surprise!

A technology blogger picked up my post, slammed my opinions, and reposted his criticism across all of his platforms. If I had not been on Google+, I would have totally missed the viral storm of comments and hateful criticisms that flooded my Inbox. At first—to be totally honest—I was terrified. I reached out to some folks I respect, and after reviewing the situation, they laughed and told me that I must be doing something right if a blogger picked up my blog. WHAT? Not normally the one in the spotlight, I managed well through it, but that was a good lesson for me and validated that what we write can be found and reposted by someone bigger and louder on today's social platforms.

I have also had the pleasure of having my blog picked up by national and international expert sources. Fox News, PR Daily to name a couple. When that happens, the traffic to your site can be overwhelming. Again, it is about being found online. The power of digital for today's business is unlimited. It amazes me when I hear C-suite leadership say that social media is a trend and doesn't matter. Trust me, it most certainly does matter, and we see the benefits for our clients daily.

SEO, search engine optimization, is critical to success for businesses and is how some of the small startups and entrepreneurs have made it big. The path to having that voice hinges on the ability to get good press, establish a digital footprint early, and maintain content creation. That's why blogging is so important. And the media reads our blogs.

If something big, relevant, or important happens in my field, I usually go to my blog to write about it. Blending the digital with traditional is the best recipe for success in my experience.

Another interesting dynamic is that the social tools are changing the way traditional media covers news. I think fallout from tweets, lack of fact-finding, and the pressure to be first at the risk of not being right all have future consequences for our industry and will probably be the subject of discussion—if not already—in journalism classes.

CHAPTER 12

Rebound from the Roadblocks

"Even before I went to the UN, I often would want to say something in a meeting—only woman at the table— and I'd think, 'OK well, I don't think I'll say that. It may sound stupid.' And then some man says it, and everybody thinks it's completely brilliant, and you are so mad at yourself for not saying something."

MADAME SECRETARY MADELEINE ALBRIGHT

ANNE

My decision to expand my business was made easier by having a retainer client at the time of transition. That was a financial safety net for me. I was able to comfortably ramp up my office presence, because I knew I had several clients who were long-term relationships. To this point, my roadblocks were manageable— a client wanting more edits, a printer second-guessing a press-check, a reporter misquoting my client.

Nine months into a one-year agreement, my retainer client decided that he would use in-house resources. The CEO had invited me to lunch at the country club. I'll never forget the scenario. I was eating my salad when he said they felt that the arrangement wasn't working out as they had envisioned, and he wanted to end the contract. I physically felt sick. I struggled to keep my game face on and finish my salad. Deep inside I just wanted to politely excuse myself and leave.

My mind started wandering while he spoke: Did this mean they don't like my work or the work arrangement? Does this mean I should move back to my home office? How could he be so thrilled with our work one day and release us the next? What signals did I miss? I got an F for emotional resilience at this lunch, but I didn't cry.

It was a serious roadblock, but it was a more threatening roadblock *mentally* than financially. After I pulled myself together, I realized that now I really had to make my business thrive, because I had a three-year commitment with a commercial landlord. No turning back.

That roadblock proved to be one of my strongest incentives in revisiting what my core services were and delivering them with excellence, precision, and to the best of my abilities. What did I learn? It wouldn't be my last roadblock, but I learned the power of emotional resilience begins in your own mind. **Nothing is ever as bad as it seems or as good as you believe.** Since that lunch, the CEO has revisited our work arrangement several times in the past five years, and I had lunch with him last week. We are working on some new projects. Roadblocks make you stronger.

In another instance, I was invited to pitch to a potential new client for a branding campaign. We were one of three firms to have an hour in front of the CEO and her board of directors—ten men and two women. The other firms pitching against us were larger, but we felt confident that our passion and creative ideas would be a good match.

We spent nearly a week of non-billable time preparing for the mock branding campaign roll-out and even handed out Cookies by Design cookies that were lettered in icing: *Big Numbers Go Down Easier with Big Cookies.* This client was a bank that was reinventing and rebranding itself. The timeline was tight and the budget was fixed.

We felt honored to have even been included in the request and gave it a great shot. After some deliberation, the board chose the larger firm, because they felt they had the manpower to deliver the campaign within the tight timeline.

I was proud of my team and thanked the bank for allowing us to be a part of the proposal process. It was a roadblock for us, and we were disappointed. But from several of these presentation experiences, I have learned that it's always best to leave a positive memory. Good marketing relationships revolve around strong personal relationships. I wished all parties well.

Shortly after that, I had the opportunity to include the female bank CEO in a public relations pitch to our business journal. I had presented an idea for a feature article on women in business and the bank CEO was a perfect fit. I included her because it made the story better. They were not my client, I wasn't paid for the PR effort, and it was something that the winning agency was responsible for.

The bank CEO was featured prominently in the article and was so impressed by our continued willingness to pitch big ideas, that she began looking for ways we could work together. After the initial branding and campaign launch, the relationship between the bank and the original agency hit a snag. They eventually asked us to be their marketing partner, and we remain their Chief Storyteller and marketing/PR firm. What was an earlier roadblock proved to be the perfect segue to a long-term relationship.

AMY

We all have roadblocks in life—divorce, failure, bankruptcy, reputation damage, public embarrassment, and illness. We have experienced some of these ourselves, and you just have to get back on your game. If you don't fail sometimes, you don't learn. I don't like to fail and neither does Anne. I think you lessen the risk of failure by watching others and reading.

The biggest roadblock I have had in owning my business was having a business partner who bailed on me just before the recession started in 2007. We were 50-50 partners and the disruption in business yielded a front-page story in the local paper. Nothing like having bad PR aimed right at you. I remember getting an email from a competitor that said: "don't bleed … the sharks are all around you." We had a lease, employees, and considerable debt we had run up building our firm. When she abruptly moved out of the state to take a corporate job, she also took our most seasoned employee with her. No, I did not see it coming. We had our differences, but her sharp turn went undetected by me until she was standing in my office telling me her last day would be within 30 days. She was the administrative partner, and I was the partner that generated most of our revenue. What this meant was I was going to have to shift fast and all of the administrative functions of running our firm were about to be heaped into my domain.

Fortunately for me, failing at what I created in the first place was not an option. I shifted into higher gear and called my banker and my CPA and got my plan together. I got out of my office lease and saved enough money to buy a commercial condo in the historic South Main arts district and moved downtown. I paid off all of our partnership-accumulated debt, along with legal and accounting fees, and focused on rebuilding my brand. I shed work we had taken on that I didn't want and hand picked the clients I wanted to keep and promote. I worked harder than ever and personally handled every client account that year. I also worked hard at developing new business and identifying new opportunities for efficiency in delivering our services to clients. What I learned is that I was happier and getting financially healthier by the day. It taught me the value of really good counsel, the importance of having a plan, and the backbone to stay the course and execute it.

The better prepared you are, the less likely you will fail. This means you have to commit to doing the hard stuff like financial planning. Making wise decisions based on facts. You don't open an office in Texas just because you want to (yes, I want to). You must have a reason. Owning a business is as much about what you cannot do as what you can do. The same is true in a career. I would not be where I am today had it not been for having to do a lot of tedious grunt work and overcoming obstacles.

Here are 9 tips for rebounding from roadblocks:

1. Surround yourself with a good support team of family, friends, and church.
2. Exercise. It's a habit of successful and productive people.
3. Read books written by smart people, and then review them on your blog.
4. Don't dwell on failure. Learn, forget, and move forward.
5. Find a mentor and listen to him/her.
6. Spend money on good financial advisors and bankers.
7. Stay in the strong zone. Play to your strengths and lead with your strengths.
8. Promote others, and be quick to recognize and leverage others' talents.
9. Share your success stories. Tell your story; write history!

CHAPTER 13
Get Uncomfortable and Grow

"Smart women are tired of working for others."

NINA L. KAUFMAN, 85 BROADS

ANNE

Women in high gear are committed to self-improvement and eager for the next opportunity. For years I had been talking to mentors and friends about growing my business to the next level. One of my favorites is a trailblazing CEO of a catering company. Jen Delaye, of JDK Catering and Event Planning, is more than a role model to Pennsylvania's women in business; she's a high-level thinker and survivor of many setbacks.

Over coffee one day, I was mentioning my hopes of finding office space, and she replied, "Haven't we had this conversation before, Anne? It's time to do it!" I was glad for her honesty and call to accountability. It was my time to stretch and commit to growing to the next level and quit talking about it. I called a realtor that day.

Getting uncomfortable might mean you map a five-year operational plan and set hiring goals and new client goals. Plan to attend two new conferences that help you forge influential, national connections. For me, when I saw *The Wall Street Journal's* Women in the Economy conference advertised, the speaker lineup was world-class. The opportunity to meet and establish a relationship with these executive women and members of *The Wall Street Journal's* editorial team could have high gear opportunities. The cost for the three-day event was in the $5,000 range. I already value investing in professional development, so the cost was not an obstacle.

The event was Invitation Only, which sends the message that this high-powered exclusive task force was not for everyone. I applied and was accepted. The value I received by meeting, listening, and talking with Madeleine Albright, Ella Edmondson, Dan Akerson, Alan Murray, Sue Shellenbarger, Dr. Gail Rosseau, and Carol Bartz was business currency.

My most recent "get-uncomfortable-and-grow" experience was my decision to expand my business into Nashville, Tennessee. From our PR and social media successes with my youngest son, Benjamin, a singer/songwriter who lives in Nashville and attends college at Belmont University, I realized that we could leverage our skills to the artist and entertainment world. And our experience with marketing in the health care industry would be a good fit for opportunities in Nashville, the nation's health care capital.

As a board member of the Harrisburg Regional Chamber, I asked our President, Dave Black, if he knew a connection at the Nashville Chamber. He introduced me to Nancy Eisenbrandt, COO, by email. From that step, I planned a flight and visited with Helen Gaye Brewster and Alison C. Lynch of the Nashville Chamber team. They were full of energy and embraced me with open arms. I may be the only Pennsylvania member of the Nashville Chamber, but I believe strongly in the work and value of chambers.

The first impression I want to leave with any potential clients in Music City is that I'm invested in your community, and I want to grow with you. My $500 membership fee is a great first step in my networking adventure down south.

In my list of role models is Marissa Mayer, CEO of Yahoo! No doubt she has met innumerable obstacles and challenges to her leadership rise and transition from Google VP to Yahoo! CEO. In an opinion piece she wrote for *BusinessWeek* in 2006, she said, "Constraints shape and focus problems, and provide clear challenges to overcome, as well as inspiration. Creativity loves constraints, but they must be balanced with a healthy disregard for the impossible."

To reach your next high gear, you'll benefit from the steps we discuss here, but you'll also need a lifetime vaccination of a *healthy disregard for the impossible*. Getting uncomfortable is the best thing you can do to reach your next high gear!

AMY

Going outside of my comfort zone is one of the most difficult things for me and has always been a challenge. I have learned to grasp what is uncomfortable with good counsel and help from those trailblazers before me. Certainly quitting the safety of full-time employment to start my own consulting business was the most uncomfortable thing I have done, followed by a few others that I have already mentioned in this book.

I think one thing that is important to stress is that there are different definitions of uncomfortable. For some, just speaking up in a meeting could be considered uncomfortable. For me, not speaking up would be more uncomfortable. I challenge you to find what is uncomfortable, and try it in the positive sense. Public speaking is uncomfortable for me, yet I force myself to do it because it helps my brand. Now, as a result of practice, it's not so uncomfortable anymore. The more I speak, the more clients I attract.

Another thing that I have learned is to ignore negative, jealous people. The higher you go, the more people will try and take you down. Don't let them. It's uncomfortable at first to have people who don't really know you say mean things and hate you for your success. Remember these words: that is their problem, not yours. I have had to endure snarky, mean, hateful public comments and have grown from it. I have reached high gear and that means I don't care what the haters think, and they won't stop me from doing what I do best. High gear women know they cannot please everyone. We know we are targets sometimes, but we shift fast and find ways to move out of that bull's-eye. And high gear women will make enemies in business, but just as we are judged by the company we keep, we are also judged by the company we don't keep. Ignore the negative.

Finally, being on television is uncomfortable for me, but this year I was invited on the Fox News Tech Take Live show via Skype. To be honest, I was not comfortable doing it, but after it was over I was happy that I had not turned down such a wonderful opportunity! High gear women know that if you must swim to the ship, you must jump in the deep end first.

Afterword

We hope our stories of our own business twists and turns will be a game changer for you. Whatever stage you find yourself in—first job, mid-career, off-ramp, relaunch, on-ramp, second career, community volunteer—we hope your high gear is squarely in your sights.

Have a story to share? We're never too busy disregarding the impossible to learn from and help another sojourner! Visit us at www.womeninhighgear.com to keep in touch.

10 Tips to Shift into High Gear

BY ANNE DEETER GALLAHER

1. **Build "up" your network.** Assemble a personal board of directors to tap for business advice. Look for trusted, well-respected C-level leaders who will help you formulate a strategy of progression to the corner office. If you are the leader of your professional network and are the most knowledgeable and experienced in your group, it's time to enlarge the circle of influence. "Your success, not only in climbing the ladder but in building a leading company, is as strong as the people you can call upon, because these are the people who will advise you, help you out, and whom you can appoint to key positions in your company in the future. As you start to get up higher in the pyramid, you realize that your networking ability, and your worth to the entire network, is what provides the keys to the kingdom," said Bill Swanson, CEO of Raytheon (*There's No Elevator to the Top*, Ramakrishnan, p. 87).

2. **Evolve from tactical manager to strategic leader.** Arriving in the corner office demands the vision of a "big picture" person. This is difficult for entrepreneurs who are accustomed to doing every detail in the business. To grow, you will have to delegate and trust your employees to do what you've trained and empowered them to do. "Develop a broad systems perspective," said Dr. Kim S. Phipps, President, Messiah College. Have a big picture for how your skills are developing. "Never chase a position, follow a development path," said James D. Dymski, Director Oncology Access, Reimbursement & Distribution at Boehringer Ingelheim.

3. **Be known for getting things done.** Idea people and innovators are critical to the lifeblood of business, but the gifted strategist assembles the perfect team to make things happen. Be that person. John Quincy Adams said, "If your actions inspire others to dream more, learn more, do more, and become more, you are a leader."

4. **Be a people broker.** Whom do you know? More importantly, who knows you? Be sure the right people know you and know that you can be trusted and depended on in all situations. "I know how important people are to your business. Whether it's on the golf course, at a sporting event, or on a board, I often refer skilled individuals to my colleagues and executive peers," said Richard E. Jordan II, CEO and Chairman of the Board, Smith Land & Improvement Corporation and L.B. Smith Ford Lincoln Inc.

5. **Be an expert communicator.** Can you communicate clearly and persuasively to people? A CEO cannot do everything herself; her communication skills and emotional intelligence will be invaluable to attract an impressive and committed group of foot soldiers.

6. **Cultivate a reputation for a strong value system and a strong work ethic—imperative qualities for the C-suite.** "Work to the position above you. People will notice!" said Kelly S. Lieblein, Vice President, Highmark Inc.

7. **Cultivate intellectual horsepower and emotional intelligence.** Regardless of your academic pedigree—Ivy, state, technical, private, community—a diploma shows the working world that you can set goals and achieve them. What you do with that acquired knowledge is what really matters as you rise the ranks

of leadership. Your ability to listen, persuade, negotiate, and respect others are core leadership capabilities.

8. **Gain a solid financial understanding.** Understand the bottom line, and how to read balance sheets. Understand profitability and cash flow, and how to reach maximum productivity for your department or company.

9. **Make time for a robust life.** "We expect our employees to live robust lives. We want to support them in their Ironman contests, their children's sports achievements, through their Scout troops, and in their musical pursuits," said Thomas F. (Chip) Brown, President, McClure Company. "If someone has to lose their marriage to be successful, then I don't want to be a leader in that organization. And I don't want to create a business environment that requires those sort of trade-offs," said Walter Bettinger, CEO, The Charles Schwab Corporation, (*There's No Elevator to the Top*, Ramakrishnan, p. 161).

10. **Accept responsibility and have a deeper concern for being respected than for being well liked.** The best leaders engender significant respect and support from their employees, not by leading with consensus, but by leading with decision-making authority. "To me consensus seems to be: the process of abandoning all beliefs, principles, values, and policies in search of something in which no one believes, but to which no one objects; the process of avoiding the very issues that have to be solved, merely because you cannot get agreement on the way ahead. What great cause would have been fought and won under the banner 'I stand for consensus'?" said Margaret Thatcher (*The Downing Street Years*, p. 167).

"Our doubts are traitors,
And make us lose the good we oft might win
By fearing to attempt."
William Shakespeare, "Measure for Measure," Act 1 scene 4
Greatest English dramatist & poet (1564 –1616)

The Birth of *Women in High Gear*

Sometimes in life you are lucky enough to meet a kindred spirit who shares an enthusiasm, passion, and power of positivity that is contagious. We joke about our North-South connection, but our serendipitous meeting on Twitter in 2009 has led to many in-real-life meetups and even projects together. It has changed our businesses and the company we keep.

On a train ride from New York City to Harrisburg, we realized that we had a lot of stories to share, and we believed our experiences could benefit others, particularly women, who were anxious to learn how to reach high gear.

Thanks to Mark Ragan, CEO of Ragan Communications, for inviting us to attend his Social Media Conference at NASDAQ that day, and ultimately ringing the closing bell at the markets on April 8, 2011. On the Amtrak train, we framed the content for this book and our challenge has been to limit it to 13 chapters.

We hope you find our experiences helpful and valuable as you chart your journey to high gear. Keep going, make your mark, and be the best you can be!

Anne & Amy

Acknowledgements

ANNE DEETER GALLAHER

Nothing in my high gear journey would have been possible without the love and faith of my parents, Edmund M. Deeter Jr. and Suzanne P. Deeter.

To Dad, thank you for your unwavering support in everything I did and your belief in "Nothing ventured, nothing gained." Thank you for teaching your children and grandchildren to love great books and to help others. You lived Abraham Lincoln's principle of "lift[ing] people out of their everyday selves and into a higher level of performance, achievement, and awareness." You are deeply missed.

And to Mother, I am so thankful that you're able to see and share in the adventures of my high gear. You have always been my biggest cheerleader.

To my husband and high school sweetheart, Corey. Who knew where high gear would take us? I couldn't make this journey without your love and support!

And to our three sons, Joshua, Aaron, and Benjamin. Your lives have made my high gear possible. Before you, I never would have believed the Lord could open such doors. You have blessed me beyond measure!

To my siblings and mentors, Edmund, Philip, and Lisa. How many questions about running a business; how many questions about surviving in business? How many times did you talk me off the ledge? You are my best friends and kindred spirits. I'm grateful for your love, honesty, and laughter. God bless you all.

To my daughter-in-law Mallary, future daughter-in-law Samantha, and your generation: We trust you'll find your challenges and obstacles easier to overcome and high gear will bring education, growth, and prosperity beyond expectation.

A very special shout out to Marisa S. Corser, my first employee and fellow sojourner on this high gear. Your support, research, critical eye, and gentle spirit have enabled me to take us to amazing heights with amazing clients! With deep respect, #YouRock!

To my personal board of advisors and to all my clients, without your belief in my work there would be no business success and certainly no high gear. I am eternally grateful for the privilege to tell your stories and to consider you my friends.

AMY D. HOWELL

To my parents, Joe and Kay Donaho, I say thank you from the core of my being for all that you taught me, the importance of faith and belief in God, and the love you have always given freely and without limits. Thank you for being sure I could do anything I wanted with an English major! You both are the best role models, and the confidence you instilled in me has allowed me to pursue my passions.

To my two younger sisters who told me I was bossy growing up, I say it must have been part of my DNA as I was seeking high gear then and didn't realize it. Thank you for putting up with big sister!

To my wonderful husband Jim Howell—CFO, father, and great partner who supports my endeavors and often spontaneous meetings with Twitter friends—I love you!

To my kids, Bryan and Abby, you are the greatest accomplishment of my life and a joy daily. My wish for you both is happiness and a high gear life in all the right ways.

To Lacey Washburn and Kiersten Bagley, thank you for allowing me to enter this next phase of high gear, and I'm enjoying sharing it with you both.

And last but never least, to all of my fabulous clients and mentors, you are the reason I am able to write this book for it is your experiences that have forged the journey!